MAX notes®

Ernest Hemingway's

The Sun Also Rises

Text by
Connie Hunter-Gillespie
(M.E., Miami University)
Department of English
Connersville High School
Connersville, Indiana

Illustrations by
Richard Fortunato

Research & Education Association

MAXnotes® for
THE SUN ALSO RISES

Printed in the United States of America

Library of Congress Catalog Card Number 96-67408

International Standard Book Number 0-87891-049-2

MAXnotes® is a registered trademark of
Research & Education Association, Piscataway, New Jersey 08854

What **MAXnotes**® *Will Do for You*

This book is intended to help you absorb the essential contents and features of Ernest Hemingway's *The Sun Also Rises* and to help you gain a thorough understanding of the work. The book has been designed to do this more quickly and effectively than any other study guide.

For best results, this **MAXnotes** book should be used as a companion to the actual work, not instead of it. The interaction between the two will greatly benefit you.

To help you in your studies, this book presents the most up-to-date interpretations of every section of the actual work, followed by questions and fully explained answers that will enable you to analyze the material critically. The questions also will help you to test your understanding of the work and will prepare you for discussions and exams.

Meaningful illustrations are included to further enhance your understanding and enjoyment of the literary work. The illustrations are designed to place you into the mood and spirit of the work's settings.

The **MAXnotes** also include summaries, character lists, explanations of plot, and section-by-section analyses. A biography of the author and discussion of the work's historical context will help you put this literary piece into the proper perspective of what is taking place.

The use of this study guide will save you the hours of preparation time that would ordinarily be required to arrive at a complete grasp of this work of literature. You will be well prepared for classroom discussions, homework, and exams. The guidelines that are included for writing papers and reports on various topics will prepare you for any added work which may be assigned.

The **MAXnotes** will take your grades "to the max."

Dr. Max Fogiel
Program Director

Contents

Section One: *Introduction* 1

    The Life and Work of Ernest Hemingway 1

    Historical Background 2

    Master List of Characters 3

    Summary of the Novel 5

    Estimated Reading Time 7

> **Each Chapter includes List of Characters, Summary, Analysis, Study Questions and Answers, and Suggested Essay Topics.**

Section Two: *Book I* 8

    Chapter 1 8

    Chapter 2 13

    Chapter 3 16

    Chapter 4 21

Chapters 5-6 25

Chapter 7 30

Section Three: *Book II* 36

Chapter 8 36

Chapter 9 41

Chapters 10-11 44

Chapter 12 50

Chapter 13 54

Chapters 14-15 59

Chapter 16 67

Chapter 17 72

Chapter 18 77

Section Four: *Book III* 83

Chapter 19 83

Section Five: *Sample Analytical Paper Topics* 90

Section Six: *Bibliography* 94

Introduction

The Life and Work of Ernest Hemingway

Ernest Hemingway was born in Oak Park, Illinois, in 1899 to Dr. and Mrs. Clarence Hemingway. His mother was musically gifted and religious, but he did not follow his mother's musical ambitions for him. Rather, he shared his father's interests in hunting and fishing. In school he took up boxing.

He began his journalism career in 1917. During World War I, he fought in the Italian infantry. Sustaining serious wounds caused him to treasure life, fear death, and handle himself well in the face of danger. He was a Red Cross ambulance driver until he was wounded. He returned home after falling in love and being rejected by the nurse who cared for him.

In 1921, Hemingway married for the first time and went to Paris where he joined a coterie of other literary minds, including Ezra Pound, Edna St. Vincent Millay, John Dos Passos, F. Scott Fitzgerald, Gertrude Stein, and others. His first book, *Three Stories and Ten Poems*, was published in Paris in 1923. During this time he also frequented Spain and became familiar with bullfights and fiestas, which later provided material for books.

In 1926 he divorced his first wife and married again the next year. With publication of *The Sun Also Rises* in 1926, Hemingway became a distinguished writer of his time. This book was declared the voice of the "lost generation."

In the 1930s, Hemingway settled in Key West and later Cuba, but still traveled to Spain, Italy, and Africa. He published several novels during this decade. In 1940, he divorced his second wife and married his third. In 1945, he divorced his third wife and married for a final time in 1946.

In 1953 he won the Pulitzer Prize for *The Old Man and the Sea,* his most popular work. In 1954 he won the Nobel Prize in Literature "for his powerful, style-forming mastery of the art of narration." He has been named one of the most powerful influences on the American short story and novel.

In 1960 he was institutionalized for bouts of paranoia and depression and received electroshock treatments. They were unsuccessful, though, and he committed suicide in Ketchum, Idaho, in 1961. His father had also committed suicide.

Historical Background

When Hemingway went to Paris in 1921, he experienced a culture shock. Gertrude Stein's phrase "lost generation" referred to the prevalent attitude of the day. The phrase came into usage because "all maps were useless and…they had to explore a new-found land for themselves—this generation was lost" (Mizener 122). In essence, these people could accept nothing about current attitudes.

They wanted to begin over through experience to work out a code of conduct to live by and respect. Members of the Jazz Age included painters, writers, rioters, artists, and the idle rich all living decadent lives. These people were American expatriates who had come to Paris as a haven for creativity and Bohemian lifestyles.

Actually, many were escaping conservative American attitudes. After World War I, politicians seemed untrustworthy, and Prohibition was politically popular. There was an upsurge of fundamentalist ministers, book and movie censorship, and groups like the KKK. Paris streets, in contrast, were filled with silent movie stars, beautiful people, and lots of liquor.

Days of cars, installment loans, and refrigerators had changed women's roles, too. They now sported short skirts, sheer dresses, bobbed hair, and lipstick. Instead of binding their waists, they now bound their breasts. This was the first generation of women to drink, smoke, dance wildly, and deal with marital problems by divorce.

Paris provided those quick divorces and diversions for this "lost generation." Writers of the time had "energy and optimism" (Mizener, 122). They were idealists who scorned conservative, American attitudes. They were dissatisfied with their own country and preferred to live elsewhere. It is said all writers eventually passed through Paris because the European world allowed them "to discover the possibilities in themselves as Americans" (Mizener, 124).

Master List of Characters

Jake Barnes—*narrator; World War I American veteran; newspaper editor from Kansas City living abroad; impotent due to a war injury.*

Robert Cohn—*Jewish; from a wealthy family; 34; mediocre writer; has difficulty with women.*

Lady Ashley (Brett)—*Jake's love; 34; is married to Lord Ashley but getting a divorce; has several affairs; an alcoholic.*

Bill Gorton—*Jake's fishing/bullfighting buddy he meets in Spain; writer.*

Mike Campbell—*Brett's fiance; rich but on an allowance; an alcoholic.*

Pedro Romero—*aficiónado; 19-year-old bullfighter; has affair with Brett.*

Juanito Montoya—*Pamplona hotel owner; passionate bullfight enthusiast.*

Frances Clyne—*Robert's girlfriend from America; uses Robert*

Marcial Lalanda—*a fading bullfighter.*

Belmonte—*a retired bullfighter who returns to the ring.*

Edna—*Bill's friend from Biarritz who parties in Pamplona.*

Mr. and Mrs. Braddocks—*Robert's literary friends.*

Harvey Stone—*a bum friend of Jake's; writer.*

Wilson Harris—*an Englishman staying in Burguete.*

Georgette Hobin—*a prostitute with Jake in Paris.*

Count Mippipopolous—*kind; well-to-do Greek who drinks and parties with Brett.*

Robert Prentiss—*a rising novelist with the Braddocks in Paris.*

Vincente Girones—*a man who is gored and killed by a bull.*

Lett—*a homosexual who comes to the Bal with Brett and dances with Georgette.*

Spider Kelly—*Robert Cohn's boxing coach; only mentioned in book.*

Zizi—*a Greek portrait painter at the Cafe Select in Paris.*

Charlie Blackman—*Edna's friend from Chicago; just mentioned in the story.*

Woolsey and Krum—*reporters from the Paris press conference.*

Madame Duzinell—*the concierge in Jake's Paris flat.*

Don Manuel Orquito—*the fireworks king.*

Tourists from Montana (unnamed except for son Hubert)—*on train to Spain.*

Madame Lavigne—*proprietress/hostess/waitress at Foyot's Restaurant.*

Mr. and Mrs. Aloysius Kirby—*send Jake a wedding announcement.*

Katherine Kirby—*daughter who is getting married.*

Patronne's Daughter—*owner of Cafe Select's daughter who fights with Georgette.*

Liaison Colonel—*man in the war who came to see Jake after his war injury.*

George—*barman at the Hotel Crillon.*

Robert's Secretary—*worked on the magazine with Robert left her for Frances.*

Paula—*woman who was supposed to meet Frances for lunch.*

Baron Mumms—*Count's friend who makes wine.*

Henry—*Count's chauffeur.*

Madame Lecomte—*proprietor of Paris restaurant on Women's Club list.*

Priest on Pilgrimage—*Catholic priest on train on pilgrimage to Rome.*

Basque—*peasant on bus.*

Bryan—*author Bill refers to.*

Raphael—*bullfight critic with Pedro.*

Algabeno—*bullfighter hurt in Madrid.*

Maid—*at Hotel Montana in Madrid.*

Summary of the Novel

The novel opens with an introduction to Robert Cohn, an insecure Jewish man whose relationships with women have lead to disastrous affairs. After his divorce, he meets Frances, who convinces him to travel to Europe. After three years with her, Cohn has written a novel, goes to America, and gets it accepted by a publisher. While he is there, attention from other women raises his confidence and makes him lose interest in Frances.

After he returns to Europe, his dissatisfaction with his life grows when he becomes smitten with Brett, a woman with whom Jake is also in love. She and Jake can never move beyond a platonic relationship, though, because of a war injury that left Jake impotent.

Robert changes when he falls in love with Brett. He no longer cares about tennis, sends Frances away, and has conflicts with people. Brett and Robert have an affair in San Sebastian, and Jake begins to despise Robert.

The group decides to go to Spain to fish. Bill, Robert, and Jake go ahead to get equipment and rooms and plan for Brett and Mike to join them later in Pamplona. Robert nervously awaits Brett's arrival. He goes to the station in case she shows up. When she does not, he does not go fishing in case Brett went to San Sebastian to meet him. Robert disgusts Bill and Jake. They go to Burguete and fish for five days before returning.

When they go to Pamplona, they stay at the Hotel Montoya, which is owned by Juanito Montoya. He respects Jake because of his passion, or *afición*, for bullfighting. The hotel is the meeting place for a*ficionados* and has pictures of only *aficiónado* bullfighters on the wall.

In Pamplona, Robert follows Brett constantly. The first day of the fiesta, streets become crowded with people drinking and partying. Releasing the bulls signals the beginning of the bullfights.

The next day the bullfights begin. Montoya introduces Bill and Jake to Romero, the newcomer. They are impressed with him as an *aficiónado*. At the bullfight, spectators are impressed with his skills, but Brett with his attractiveness. Brett soon falls for Romero

The next day Romero steals the show. Montoya shows his protectiveness for Romero when the American ambassador wants Romero to join him for coffee. Montoya expresses concern that this attention may spoil Romero. Jake agrees and suggests Montoya lose the message. However, when Brett insists on being introduced and confides to Jake she has fallen in love with Romero, Jake violates his *afición* and arranges their affair.

When Jake returns to the group without Brett, Robert panics. When Robert finds Brett is with Romero, Robert calls Jake a "pimp" as he hits him. Robert finds Brett in Romero's room and nearly kills him, but Romero does not quit. After Brett lambasts him, Robert begins crying and apologizes to Romero and later to Jake. He leaves Pamplona in the morning.

The next morning is the final day of the fiesta. As bulls are running the streets into the ring, one man gets gored. The president's attendance brings pomp and circumstance. Brett, radiantly in love with Romero, sits with Jake and Bill at the bullring. She shows adoration and concern for Romero although she says his people disapprove of her. Romero hands his gold-brocade cape to his sword-handler to give to Brett.

Belmonte, the first fighter, kills his bull without much drama. Romero fights next. He works perfectly, though he is still injured from Robert's beating. The bull does not see well, and the crowd wants another bull. Marcial fights next, and the crowd responds ecstatically.

Romero's last bull is the one that had killed the man. He works smoothly and efficiently at both killing the bull and pleasing the crowd. He gives the ear to Brett.

After the bullfight, the fiesta winds down. Brett leaves with Romero, and everyone else goes his own way. Jake stays one night in Bayonne before leaving for San Sebastian. After three days he

Introduction

receives cables from Brett that she is in Madrid and needs help.

When Jake arrives, Brett cries and tells him she sent Romero away because she knew she was no good for him. He had been ashamed of her. Romero had offered her money, but she could not take it. She decides to go back to Mike. As the story ends, she bemoans that she and Jake could have been good together. Jake realizes it is only a nice dream.

The novel, written in a narrative frame, is divided into three books. Book I includes Chapters 1–7 and is set in Paris. This is often considered Hemingway's wasteland, which represents the lifestyle of the "lost generation." It builds main characters and ends with Brett going off to San Sebastian for a liaison with Robert.

Book II includes Chapters 8–18 and is set in Spain, the possible corrective values for Paris' lifestyle. Here, the group goes for fishing and bullfighting. Here Jake demonstrates then violates his values. There is still lots of drinking and sex. At the end of the book, Brett has left for a liaison with Romero.

Book III includes only Chapter 19, is still set in Spain, and is winding down. The fiesta is over and there is no more partying. The focus in this chapter is on Jake, who goes off without any of his friends to regain his values. He is called to Madrid at the end. Although the novel begins with development of Robert Cohn, it ends without reference to him—as if he were obliterated from life. Brett will end with Mike.

Estimated Reading Time

An average reader can read the book in six to seven hours. A more careful reading will take longer because of unfamiliar terms and places. It is difficult to read in one sitting.

The Sun Also Rises, Book I

Chapter 1

New Characters:

Robert Cohn: *Princeton grad; Jake's tennis partner; Frances' lover*

Jake Barnes: *narrator*

Frances: *Robert's girlfriend*

Braddocks: *Robert's literary friend*

Spider Kelly: *Robert's college boxing coach; only mentioned in story*

Summary

Robert Cohn is introduced as an integral character whose life is filled with insecurities. At Princeton, he had taken up boxing as a defense mechanism for insecurities of being Jewish. He was over-matched and got his nose flattened, which made him dislike boxing but like the power his skill could give him. No one from school remembers him.

His shyness made him marry the first girl who was nice to him. He was unhappily married, had three children, lost most of his inheritance, and ultimately was devastated when his wife deserted him.

After the divorce, he goes to California and falls among literary types. With little money, he backs an arts review publication. He is taken on by Frances, an overbearing woman wanting to rise socially. When Cohn can no longer afford the magazine, she decides to take what she can and insists on a trip to Europe so Robert can write. They stay for three years, mostly in Paris. During this time, Robert has two friends in Europe, Braddocks and Jake.

When Frances' looks begin to deteriorate, she decides Robert should marry her, since he receives a comfortable allowance of $300 per month. At this point in their relationship, her attitude changes from apathy to jealousy and possessiveness. At dinner, when Jake mentions another woman, Robert kicks him under the table so Jake will avoid the topic since Frances is so jealous. Robert decides on travel plans based on these jealousies. As they part, he worries Jake may be angry.

Analysis

From the Ecclesiastes quote that precedes Chapter 1, Hemingway has derived both his title and his theme. "One generation passeth away, and another cometh; but the earth abideth forever." Stein's "lost generation" is always in quest of something that neither Hemingway nor his characters find.

Seemingly little plot happens in this chapter, but Hemingway sets the stage for Robert's later choices. Robert is a man inadequate in most areas. As a writer, he is poor. His religion is also undesirable since he was ridiculed at Princeton and by other characters throughout the novel for being Jewish. He is physically unappealing both before and after his nose is smashed.

When Jake says the flattening "certainly improved his nose," he is referring to Robert's typically long Jewish nose. This reference to the anti-semitism of the 1920s explains Robert's feelings of inferiority and shyness because of anti-Jewish feelings in Princeton. Jake feels Cohn became good at boxing to protect himself against jeering and insults. No one remembers him as a boxer, however, probably because his faith made him insignificant to his classmates.

Robert is equally inept with women. First, he marries because his wife pays attention to him, but he cannot keep her happy. Then, he is a failure as a man with Frances, who assumes the lead in their relationship. In this chapter, when he gets attention from women because of his writing and later when Brett sleeps with him, he does not put that attention into perspective. His lack of social skills makes him see these things as more important than they are.

He is unable to be assertive, not only with women but also with men. He only has two friends and alienates his acquaintances. He is insecure enough to make decisions based on if Frances is jealous or if Jake is offended. Later, when he fights with Jake and others, he does not see his indignation as justified but rather begs their forgiveness.

Robert's relationship with Frances demonstrates his personality throughout the book. Frances is the leader, Robert the follower. She wants Robert for companionship and the security that he can give her and does not display a desire for him except as it will benefit her.

Frances, and later more obviously Brett, represents the "lost generation," which had departed from traditional moral values. For example, she lives with Robert while not married. She lives with him for her own betterment rather than out of love. She lives a wild life of partying. Her actions demonstrate selfish motivations rather than thoughts of what others need.

At this point, Hemingway has presented two women and both negatively. Of the four main women in the novel, three are drunks who are free sexually. Even Robert's wife is not long-suffering but rather leaves him for another man. He also presents women who are getting divorced, a taboo idea for his time.

Robert does have some athletic prowess. He is good at football and tennis and was middleweight boxing champion in college. However, those are both temporal things since no one remembers his achievements when he gets out of college. These things also fade with age. When he later falls in love, his tennis game also suffers.

Since this chapter adds little to the plot, critics believe Hemingway wants to contrast Robert and Jake. Jake reveals Cohn's failures and ineffectiveness, presenting him as, according to Jake's standards, "unmanly" and socially impotent. This later correlates with Jake's physical impotence.

Robert is impotent of spirit—very unassertive and having little self-esteem. Jake is a "real man" in spirit but not in body. Perhaps Cohn's description is foreshadowing the impotence of values and mores that are not respected by the "lost generation." Robert represents the innocence that Jake has lost.

Jake's character unfolds later, however. Jake is surprised about Cohn's being a boxing champion. Jake loves sports, as a typical Hemingway hero, and is disgusted by anyone who does not give himself passionately into a sport. Jake has much passion, but he cannot physically give his passion to the woman he loves. He resents he is a "man" who cannot do what a man should. Cohn is "not a man" but has opportunities to do and ruins each chance.

Jake has cynical and sarcastic humor. He derides Cohn by saying his appearance was improved after his broken nose. He also subtly ridicules Cohn by saying he "took to wearing spectacles," instead of saying eyeglasses, because he read too much. This excessive reading is a flaw of Robert's because he often lives based on what he reads about rather than from first-hand experience.

Jake continues to ridicule Robert by saying he thinks "perhaps a horse stepped on Cohn's face." However, his tone becomes bitter toward Robert when he says he does not trust "frank and simple people." Robert's innocence will later make him play the foil character to Jake's cynicism.

Study Questions

1. Where did Robert attend college?

2. What is Robert's religion?

3. Who is the narrator?

4. Give three sports in which Robert excelled.

5. Why is Jake suspicious about Robert's having been a middle-weight boxing champion?

6. How many years did Robert stay in Europe?

7. Why does Frances change her attitude toward Robert?

8. What sport do Robert and Jake share?

9. What shows Frances' jealousy?

10. What shows Robert's insecurity at the end of the chapter?

Answers

1. Robert attended college at Princeton.

2. Robert is Jewish.

3. The narrator of the novel is Jake Barnes.

4. Three sports in which Robert had excelled were boxing, football, and tennis.

5. Jake is suspicious about Robert's actually having been a boxing champion at Princeton because no one from Princeton seems to remember him.

6. Robert stayed in Europe three years.

7. Frances decides Robert would be a good catch because her looks are going.

8. Robert and Jake enjoy playing tennis together.

9. Frances becomes jealous of Robert when Jake mentions a girl in Strasbourg.

10. At the end of Chapter 1, Robert is afraid Jake is angry with him.

Suggested Essay Topics

1. Describe Robert's experiences with women. Why was he devastated by his divorce? How has Frances affected his life? How has their relationship changed? Why? How does this prepare the way for Robert's relationship with Brett?

2. Explain why Hemingway begins the novel with this chapter. Why is Cohn important enough to describe in detail? What clues does Jake give the reader to his negative feelings toward Robert?

Chapter 2

Summary

Robert goes to America and gets his book accepted by an American publisher. While he is there, attention from several women raises his self-confidence. This also makes him lose interest in Frances, since he realizes he has something to offer women.

He reads *The Purple Land* by W. H. Hudson. This describes imaginary romantic adventures that Robert takes as gospel. These things combined make him dissatisfied with his life, so he tries to talk Jake into a trip to South America. Jake refuses because he not only likes Paris but also goes to Spain in the summer.

Jake and Robert go for a drink. Robert regrets that his life is half over. He does not like Paris and thinks South America will cure his dissatisfaction. Jake's normal exit line to get away from Robert does not work, and he goes to the office with Jake. He sits, waits, and reads while Jake works hard for a few hours. When Jake goes to the outer office, Robert is asleep in the chair with his head in his arms.

As Robert awakens, he cries out in his sleep. He pretends it is a dream, but he says he did not sleep the night before because he and Frances were talking.

Analysis

Chapter 2 foreshadows Robert's falling so hard later for Brett. He never been in love nor has he felt he has anything to offer a woman until now. Robert wants to live life. His is half over, and he has not loved.

This chapter also contrasts Jake and Robert. Robert sees bullfighting as an "abnormal life" while Jake thinks "nobody ever lives their life all the way up except bullfighters." This appreciation for bullfighters becomes part of Jake's code later in the story.

Robert wants to live a different life; Jake is satisfied with what he is doing. Robert is not an independent thinker but rather gets his ideas from books. Jake does not.

Robert is romantic while Jake is cynical. Jake refers to Robert's romantic delusions as Robert has "it badly." Robert likes the simplicity of South America while Jake likes the glamour of

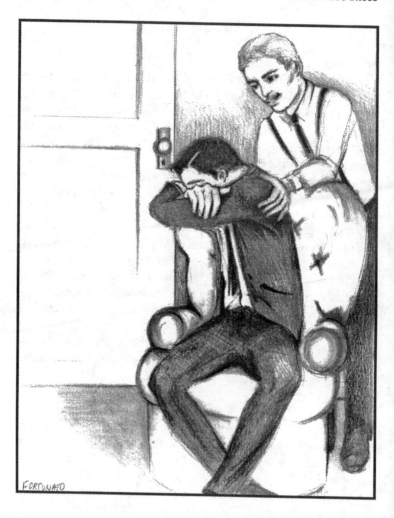

FORTUNATO

bullfighting. Jake thinks that, rather than escaping to another place, Robert should start living his life in Paris. Robert does not like Paris.

Although both men are writers to varying degrees, Robert is part of the rich who think an "important part of ethics (is) to appear not to work." Jake, on the other hand, writes on a daily basis for a living. Robert witnesses Jake working in this chapter and, in essence, sees into his soul.

This chapter also begins the trend for over-indulging in alcohol. Characters equate liquor with having fun. As many Americans in Paris at this time, they say a good bar is one having lots of liquor.

Study Questions

1. How does Robert's perception of himself with women change?

2. How old is Robert?

3. Where does he want Jake to go?

4. What is Robert sick of?

5. What book does Robert read?

6. Who does Jake think lives life to the fullest?

7. What is Jake's line when he wants to get rid of people?

8. Where does Robert get his ideas?

9. What happens when Robert waits for Jake in the office?

10. What do we know about his and Frances' relationship at the end?

Answers

1. After Robert publishes his book, he realizes he is desirable to women.

2. Robert is 34.

3. Robert wants Jake to travel with him to South America.

4. Robert is sick of Paris.

5. Robert read *The Purple Land* by Hudson.

6. Jake believes bullfighters live their lives to the fullest.

7. When Jake wants an exit line, he tells people he has to get off some cables.

8. Robert is not an original thinker and gets his ideas from books.

9. Robert falls asleep in a chair and has a nightmare while he is waiting for Jake to finish his work.

10. At the end, the reader is led to believe he and Frances are having trouble because he says they stayed up all night talking.

Suggested Essay Topics

1. Compare Jake's and Robert's views of life. Why does Robert think South America will cure his dissatisfaction? How have Robert's interests and goals been developed? Jake's?

2. Discuss this quotation: "Nobody ever lives their life all the way up except bullfighters." How does this foreshadow Jake's *afición* values? Why does Jake feel life must be lived to the fullest? How does the "lost generation" fit into this attitude?

Chapter 3

New Characters:

Georgette Hobin: *a Paris prostitute*

Mr. and Mrs. Braddocks: *Cohn's literary friends*

Brett: *Jake's friend who is a sexually free alcoholic*

Robert Prentiss: *a rising novelist with the Braddocks*

Lett: *a homosexual who comes to the Bal with Brett and dances with Georgette*

Madame Lavigne: *proprietress/hostess/waitress at Foyot's Restaurant*

Summary

After Robert leaves the Napolitain, Georgette, a prostitute, walks past and begins a conversation with Jake. They go to dinner. While they are in the cab, Georgette begins to kiss Jake and puts her hand on his genitals. He stops her by saying he is sick. He later tells her he was hurt in the war.

While she and Jake are having dinner, they meet Cohn, Frances, Mr. and Mrs. Braddocks, and several others. Jake introduces

Georgette, who instantly dislikes Frances. At dinner they discuss Paris before leaving for a dancing hall.

While Georgette is dancing, Jake gets a beer and stands in the doorway for fresh air. As he is standing there, two cabs of gay young men come in. With them is Brett, with whom Jake is in love.

The gay men decide it would be great sport to dance with Georgette since she is a true prostitute. Jake is infuriated rather than tolerant of them. He leaves as they are all taking turns. He is angry and sickened by what is happening.

Brett comes over, and Jake notices Robert staring at her. When he asks her to dance, she shows her apathy for him by first dancing with, then leaving with, Jake. Robert watches them all the time.

Jake and Brett leave in the taxi. Brett leans back in the corner of the cab with her eyes closed and says she has been miserable.

Analysis

Brett's introduction begins building relationships crucial to the outcome of the novel. Robert, who is already dissatisfied with his life, is ripe for love and instantly falls for Brett. Brett's immediate apathy toward Robert is the same response she has even after their later affair. Brett is presented as happy-go-lucky. She lets down the facade only to Jake in the cab at the end when she says she is "miserable."

Jake's being in the taxi with Georgette and Brett shows one major aspect of the novel. The characters are constantly moving about, like Hemingway's "lost generation." Throughout the novel, characters go by taxi, car, bus, or foot. This sometimes seemingly random movement represents the equally random lifestyles of the "lost generation," always moving about but never fulfilling their quest for a better world.

Paris is presented as a wasteland in its perversions. Hemingway shows values of the "lost generation" reflected in Paris, which is the entire world, and there "isn't anywhere else." Clocks in the *New York Herald* Bureau window call attention to how America is represented in Paris by expatriates who have fled in reaction to the unsatisfying norms, such as the "dirty war."

He shows a lack of traditional moral values when Georgette says, "Everybody's sick." Hemingway sees society as having an

illness, which Paris life represents. Jake reacts angrily to Prentiss'
question about seeing Paris as "amusing." His reaction is so pronounced, Prentiss responds that he wishes he "had that faculty" to
get angry. Jake's anger shows his intensity of feeling about behavior that is undesirable.

Here in this Paris wasteland, traditional values do not oper-
ate, so Jake is sickened. He "was very angry" about the homosexuals who represent one aspect of a decadent society that does not

see its own depravity. The homosexuals are infatuated with Georgette as a taboo creature, but they do not recognize their own antisocial behavior. Brett sees bringing Georgette in as an insult to the rest of them, but Jake sees Brett's coming in with the gay men the same way.

Jake's impotence parallels a society that has become impotent as a result of how they live. Both he and Brett are infertile. They cannot produce children just like this generation of lost souls cannot produce. Life is a trap with no way out. Love is not typical when Jake's date, or fiance as he calls her, is a prostitute. Jake loves Brett, but she cannot love him back because of his impotence.

Drinking plays a major part in this society. Georgette and Jake drink pernod, an imitation absinthe, like their values are imitations of real ones. Absinthe is a liqueur flavored with wormwood, a bitter aromatic green oil. Thence the term has come to mean "something bitter or grievous" (Websters), as Hemingway felt about this society.

Drunkenness accompanies illicit activities. Jake never fully participates or approves but rather stays not drunk enough to forget what is happening but "just enough to be careless." Only later when Jake is trying to forget his actions does he indulge to the point of actually being drunk.

Religion is presented in connection with Jake when Brett says, "You've a hell of a biblical name, Jake." Jake is frequently confronted with lifestyles and choices different from his Catholic background. He is wrestling with his own values, just as the biblical Jacob wrestled with the angel.

With this chapter's focus on Jake's being unable to satisfy the woman he loves, Hemingway first establishes his connection between Jake and Robert. Both are emasculated men—Jake, physically; Robert, emotionally and socially. However, Jake is unable to retrieve his manhood while Robert could.

Study Questions

1. What drink does Georgette order?

2. What is physically wrong with Georgette?

3. How did Jake get hurt?

4.   Where do Jake and the others go?

5.   What is Georgette's occupation?

6.   What city is Jake from?

7.   What does Georgette think of Paris?

8.   What type of people does Brett arrive with?

9.   Who falls for Brett at the end of the chapter?

10. How is Brett different in the taxi?

Answers

1.   Georgette orders pernod.

2.   Georgette has bad teeth.

3.   While Jake was in the war, he received his injury.

4.   Jake and the others go to the Bal, a dance club.

5.   Georgette is a prostitute.

6.   Jake is an American from Kansas City.

7.   Georgette thinks Paris is dirty and expensive.

8.   When Brett arrives at the dance club, she is with a group of gay men.

9.   At the end of the chapter, Robert is acting smitten with Brett.

10. Unlike the normal carefree exterior she presents, when Brett is in the taxi with Jake she is open and honest.

Suggested Essay Topics

1.   Show Paris as a wasteland. How are perversions of love demonstrated? How does Georgette fit into this? What is the significance of Jake's anger in the dancing club?

2.   Explain Georgette's comment, "Everybody's sick." How is this a statement on society? How does Jake's injury represent society? Are there other "sick" characters in the novel?

Chapter 4

New Characters:

Mike Campbell: *Brett's fiance; rich but on an allowance; an alco-holic*

Count Mippipopolous: *a fat count at the Cafe Select*

Zizi: *a Greek portrait painter*

Mr. and Mrs. Aloysius Kirby: *send Jake a wedding announcement*

Katherine Kirby: *daughter who is getting married*

Patronne's daughter: *owner of Cafe Select's daughter who fights with Georgette*

Madame Duzinell: *concierge in Jake's Paris flat*

Liaison colonel: *man in the war who came to see Jake after his war injury*

Summary

In the taxi, Jake kisses Brett and she pushes far away from him. When he questions her, she says she cannot stand for him to touch her because she becomes sexually aroused but cannot be satisfied because of his impotence, which was caused by a war injury. She thinks this torture is life's way of getting even with her because of the way she has treated other men.

They ride around before going to the Cafe Select. There they are reunited with their friends, except for Frances and Robert, who have left. Jake says he has a headache and returns to his room. He shows disdain for both Brett and his feelings for her. As he readies himself for bed, he reads bullfighting news. When he is in bed, he still mourns his injury and inability to perform. As he thinks about it, he cries.

After a while, he is awakened by noise. Brett is downstairs making a row to see him. She tells him the Count brought her here. He had offered her money to go away with him, but Brett had re-fused. She wants Jake to come and drink with her, but Jake says he has to work in the morning and she is too far ahead on drinks. As she leaves, Jake again feels sadness.

Analysis

In this chapter, Brett is portrayed in a mixed light. On one hand, she is a cold woman who moves as far away from Jake as she can in the taxi. This is a stark contrast to how Georgette, though a prostitute, had been passionate and warm to Jake. Jake had rejected Georgette's advances because of his impotence, and Brett rejects Jake's for the same reason. On the other hand, we see a vulnerability in Brett because of her unhappiness. She wants Jake but cannot

FORTUNATO

ever have him because of his injury. Jake feels she "only wanted what she couldn't have" and really does not love him. Her dual character is portrayed when she seems assertive and independent, although actually "she was afraid of so many things." Her facade is down with Jake when, at the end of Chapter 3, she admits to being "miserable." Jake says he can see through her exterior and "could see all the way into" her soul.

Hemingway states his theme when Brett says "…we pay for all the things we do." If Brett is correct, her unhappiness is the result of her careless attitude with men. If Jake's impotence, however, is his punishment for sins, the reader is not aware of it. Jake's later actions, though, will necessitate penance. When Brett feels she is paying for what she has put men through, the idea of a higher power doling out justice is introduced.

Later, the religious aspect is further developed when Jake mentions the Catholic church and how priests handle the inability to perform sexually. The church tells them simply "not to think about it." Jake sees that as ironic and sarcastically says that approach is unnatural.

The chapter makes many references to Jake's impotence. He says people think it is funny, like they think drunks are funny. He goes along with the joke, but the injury has devastated his life. His impotence not only makes him the object of jokes, but also makes a relationship with his love impossible, which is devastating to him. Since the injury occurred in the war, it also makes a statement against the war.

Jake acts fatalistic about it and says he is calmly accepting his injury, but then during the night his crying is anything but calm. His public image is important in many aspects, and he finds it is "easy to be hard-boiled about everything in the daytime." Night, however, is when his facade is broken.

Relationships are also important. Jake loves Brett; Brett, on the other hand, vows her love for him yet sees his inability to consummate as a pivotal aspect. She sees this as the ultimate joke and judgment for her. Because they do not have to play sexual games, though, she can be more honest with him than with other characters. He is less than honest with himself and how he feels when he says, "To hell with Brett." For Robert, his infatuation with Brett is already obvious as he is pining for her when he leaves the Cafe Select.

Since Jake's code is an important part of the novel, the mention is important. Jake walks through streets, conscious of Paris and its past, as he longs for past values no longer held. Jake's reading bullfighting news before he goes to bed foreshadows another important area of his values—bullfighting.

Unlike Jake, the Count values things he loves in the present. Brett says, "He's quite one of us" to indicate he is the idle rich Hemingway felt leery of. Codes are important to Jake and Hemingway and will be developed throughout the novel.

Study Questions

1. Why won't Brett let Jake be romantic in the taxi?

2. What does Brett feel is the reason she is unable to have Jake sexually?

3. How do other people react to Jake's injury?

4. What is Zizi's occupation?

5. Whom does Georgette get into a fight with?

6. How does Robert look when he goes home with Frances?

7. What are Jake's two pieces of mail?

8. How does Jake show intense feelings for Brett while he is alone?

9. Who is Zizi's benefactor?

10. Who is waiting for Brett in the car?

Answers

1. Brett will not let Jake get intimate in the taxi because she knows he cannot consummate their romance.

2. Brett thinks her inability to have Jake is God's way of repaying her for breaking men's hearts.

3. Other people think Jake's injury is funny.

4. Zizi is a portrait painter.

5. Georgette gets into a fight with the patronne's daughter at Bal's.

6. When Robert leaves with Frances, he looks depressed.

7. When Jake checks his mail, he has received a bank statement and a wedding announcement.

8. When Jake is alone contemplating his feelings for Brett, he cries.

9. Zizi's benefactor is Count Mippipopolous.

10. Count Mippipopolous is waiting in the car for Brett.

Suggested Essay Topics

1. Explain Brett's quote, "Don't we pay for all the things we do...? Why does Brett feel she is being punished? How? To what extent are the wounds the result of external forces?

2. How does Jake deal with his impotence? How do other people see it? Explain the quotation, "You, a foreigner...have given more than your life." Does Jake agree? How is his impotence relevant to society's?

Chapters 5–6

New Characters:

Woolsey: *a reporter from the press conference*

Krum: *a reporter from the press conference*

Harvey Stone: *an American; a drunken friend of Jake's*

George: *barman at the Hotel Crillon*

Robert's secretary: *worked on the magazine with Robert; left her for Frances*

Paula: *woman who was supposed to meet Frances for lunch*

Summary

The next morning Jake walks to his office among the working class. After putting in a good morning at work, he goes to a press conference. On the way back, he shares a taxi with a couple of other reporters. When he returns to the office, Robert is waiting. They go to a restaurant to have hors d'oeuvres and small talk. Conversation turns to Frances and how Robert has certain obligations to her. Then Robert begins to pump him about Brett.

Jake tells Robert that Brett was his nurse in the war when he was injured. She is now married to the titled Lord Ashley from

whom she is getting a divorce so she can marry Mike Campbell. Jake tries saying things about Brett to discourage Robert. Jake tells some history of how Brett was working in the hospital during the war and lost her true love. When Robert perceives Jake has insulted Brett, he gets angry.

After lunch, Jake works, but when he goes to meet Brett, she does not show up. He then goes to the Cafe Select and meets Harvey Stone, who hints for Jake to give him money. Robert shows up, and there is a conflict between he and Harvey. Robert says he is displaying signs of writer's block.

While they are waiting, Frances comes and asks Jake to join her. She tells Jake that Robert wants to leave her under pretense of getting material for a new book. She says now she will not be able to find anyone else who will have her. When they go back to Robert, she insults him mercilessly. She tells Jake about a secretary at the magazine whom Robert had dumped for Frances. Jake cannot believe Robert is taking humiliation from Frances. He leaves while Frances is still insulting Robert.

Analysis

In these chapters, Robert shows he has fallen in love with Brett and certain changes are happening. For example, Robert has "decided he hasn't lived enough." He no longer cares about tennis, he wants to leave Francis, and he has conflicts with people with whom he did not have problems before. This romance is significant for him because until he falls in love, nothing in his life makes him stand out. Brett gives him identity.

Robert's idea of romance presented in an earlier chapter is instrumental in making him fall so hard for Brett. Jake wonders if Robert really enjoys Paris but says he does not because he gets his likes and dislikes from an author named Mencken. He also says Robert has been molded by "the two women who had trained him" and now his character is to be molded by Brett or by her apathy toward him.

Frances comments on his inability to be an independent thinker when she says he does not like a writer his friends said was bad. She also notes that part of his hesitance about marrying her is for the romance of having a mistress. She observes that once they marry their relationship will no longer be the romance he longs for.

Robert is a "case of arrested development." He wants to play football, which is fine for an 18-year-old but not a 34-year-old. He just accepts Frances' humiliating him rather than being angry. This lack of character is part of the reason for conflict emerging between Jake and Robert. Robert has a "boyish sort of cheerfulness" that is the innocence Jake has lost and now resents in Robert.

Tension between Robert and Jake first is apparent where Brett is concerned. Jake resents and even discourages Robert's involvement and tells him to "go to hell." Jake says she is a drunk who is in love with Mike and is going to marry him. When Robert stands as if to hit Jake, it is the first of many times he poses a threat but does not follow through. This reaction about Brett is interesting when Robert sees Jake as his "best friend."

Harvey, who seems more like Jake's friend than Robert, is a stark contrast to Robert. Harvey is not a fighter like Robert. Robert cannot stand him and says Harvey always makes him angry and gets on his nerves. Harvey calls Robert a "moron." Although Harvey is a bum, Jake seems to like him better than Robert, which shows Robert's extreme lack of social skills. Harvey brings out Jake's gullible side when he gives Harvey money even though Harvey is lying.

Frances is another character who provides contrast to Robert. He feels obligations to Frances out of a sense of what is right. She bemoans Robert is leaving her because no one will want her now and she will have no money. She had gotten a quick divorce and not tried to profit financially thinking Robert would marry her. Jake does not sympathize with her because her motivations are self-serving.

When she does say she wants to eventually have a normal life with children, she says she really does not like children but thought she would grow to like them. This is a vivid contrast to real characters presented. Krum represents normal people who have a job, a wife, and children. Jake likes that aspect of life as he walks along with the working class and "felt pleasant to be going to work." Frances, on the other hand, represents the idle rich who want it all and hurt others in their attempt to have it.

Study Questions

1. How did Jake originally meet Brett?

2. Whom is Brett divorcing?

3. Who asks Jake for money?

4. Whom does Robert say he dislikes?

5. What does Frances want that Robert will not do?

6. What had Frances thought she would have even though she does not like them?

7. Whom did Robert leave when he met Frances?

8. Where is Robert sending Frances?

9. What reason does Robert give Frances for leaving her?

10. Why is Jake uncomfortable with the conversation between Robert and Frances?

Answers

1. Jake and Brett met in the hospital where Jake was sent for his injury during the war.

2. Brett is in the process of obtaining a divorce from Lord Ashley.

3. Harvey Stone hints to Jake he needs money.

4. Robert dislikes Harvey Stone, and the feeling is mutual.

5. Frances wants Robert to marry her, but he refuses.

6. Frances had assumed she would always have children.

7. Robert had left his secretary when he met Frances.

8. Robert is sending Frances to England to be with friends.

9. Robert tells Frances he needs to get material for a new book.

10. Jake is uncomfortable with the conversation between Frances and Robert because she is insulting Robert, and he is not standing up for himself.

Suggested Essay Topics

1. Describe the relationship between Frances and Robert. How does Frances feel his leaving her demonstrates the aspect of his character of seeking adventures through books? Why doesn't Robert defend himself? How was their relationship developed through his insecurities?

2. Contrast the normal people presented in the reading with Jake's Paris friends. How are Krum and Woolsey different from Jake's other friends? Why does Jake walk to work? How do the characters presented as normal working people contrast to Harvey Stone? Frances?

Chapter 7

New Characters:

Baron Mumms: *the Count's friend who makes wine*

Henry: *the Count's chauffeur*

Summary

Jake escapes to his hotel and finds Brett has been there. Although last night the concierge had thought Brett to be crude, today she says Brett is very gentile. After Jake showers, Brett arrives with Count Mippipopolous, who is one of her admirers.

While Jake is dressing, Brett comes in to see what is wrong with him. He again vows his love to her. Brett sends the Count away for champagne while Jake lies on the bed. He is trying to deal with his apparent arousal and love for Brett but inability to do anything about either of them. He asks her to live with him or go off to the country. Brett says she could not live in the country with anyone, even her true love. She says she cannot say she loves him even though he vows his love to her.

Brett tells him she is going to San Sebastian and refuses his offer to go along. When the Count returns with champagne, they discuss values. They go to dinner and afterward go dancing. As they are dancing, Brett realizes she has not thought about Michael for a week.

FORTUNATO

As they are dancing, Brett again admits to Jake she is miserable. Jake realizes this is the same pattern their relationship has taken in the past. Jake takes Brett home and kisses her at the door. She pushes him away in frustration; then Jake goes back to his flat.

Analysis

In this chapter the relationship between Brett and Jake comes full circle. Jake shows his adoration for her in the scene at his flat. He pitifully violates his dignity by begging Brett to live with him or go with him to the country. Just vowing his love for her degrades him since he knows how she feels about him.

Brett's saying she is miserable is a repeat of their prior conversation. Jake has the "feeling of going through something that has all happened before." There is no real progress or development in their relationship. Jake is her only friend, she says, because she jokes with other people but not him. She does not have to don falseness with him because he is not a sexual creature in her eyes. The end of Book I and the Paris wasteland is the same as the taxi scene when Jake is offering her tenderness, but she pushes him away.

She realizes Jake has an authenticity others do not. She says, "We all have titles" except Jake. Titles, either real or supposed, grant them entrance into this glittering wasteland Paris has become. Though he has no title, Jake's scars gain him entrance into this coterie of the disillusioned. He has been injured from war and is unable to perform physically.

But his scars are no more pronounced than Brett's in her inability to find love and fulfillment. Twice she has said she is miserable. She lost her love and now is marrying for the third time, as soon as her divorce is final. There is not only no mention of love for Mike, but she does not even think of him for a week.

When the Count shows scars of his wounds, she repeats he is one of them. The fact they all have been wounded in some way, especially by this generation's loss of innocence, allows them entrance into this special club.

Not only Jake but also the Count can see through Brett's facade. He says she and Jake should be together. Ironically, Brett is marrying Mike out of desperation but says she cannot marry Jake because they have their "careers." When Jake adds, "We want to lead our own lives" the lost generation's attitude toward self-fulfillment is presented. They are searching for something to fill the void left by their dissatisfaction with current conventional politics and attitudes.

The Count realizes Brett does not "need a title. You got class all over you," he tells her. He thinks she is charming when she is drunk but sees wildness as a defense mechanism. He says, "You're always drinking my dear. Why don't you just talk?" By her wildness, Brett covers her true feelings of desperation she is unwilling to share with anyone but Jake.

Though the Count does show insight into Brett, he represents the ultimate in the "lost generation's" quest for satisfying physical desires. He is a wine expert; he smokes cigars. He eats so much he is described as "very large. Very, very large." He makes his living by owning a chain of candy stores. He is a collector of antiquities. When Jake and Brett are leaving, he has three girls at his table. Whatever feels good is what the Count says is right.

The Count has established a goal of satisfying physical cravings as what he values in life. His code is he "would do it if I would enjoy it…That is the secret. You must get to know the values." The Count's values include whatever brings pleasure, and he immerses himself in that world. On the other hand, Jake values such things as the integrity that comes with work.

Jake realizes that, though they are all wounded, there is a difference. The Count has been in "seven wars and four revolutions," but his wound came on a business trip. Jake fought in the war and for his effort and integrity got wounded irreparably. Jake's wounds are serious and have affected his life forever, but his soul is intact.

Even Brett sees the Count's, i.e., her generation's, lack of integrity when she says, "You haven't any values. You're dead, that's all." She, on the other hand, is like the Count in pursuing what is pleasurable regardless of its acceptability. For example, she has been so taken with having fun this week she has neglected to think of her fiance. She also rejects Jake though he is obviously hurting for her.

Brett and the Count, both with their titles and social standing, represent the ultimate in what Hemingway is writing against. This generation has strayed from what is right.

Study Questions

1. Whom does Brett bring to Jake's flat?

2. What errand does Brett send the Count on?

3. What does Jake ask Brett to do?

4. Where does Brett say she is going?

5. Brett says she has not thought of whom in a week?

FORTUNATO

6. When the Count gets wine at the dance club, what is the year on the bottle?

7. While they are dancing, how does Jake feel about Brett's openness with him?

8. Why does Brett push Jake away at the door?

9. What do all the things the Count values have in common?

10. What does the Count think of Zizi?

Answers

1. Brett brings Count Mippipopolous to Jake's flat.

2. Brett sends Count Mippipopolous to get champagne so she can talk to Jake.

3. Jake asks Brett to live with him or go with him to the country.

4. Brett tells Jake she is going to San Sebastian.

5. Brett has not thought of Michael, her fiancé, in a week.

6. The year on the wine bottle is 1811.

7. When Brett is open with him while dancing, Jake feels he has been through that before.

8. Brett pushes Jake away at the door because he is kissing her.

9. All of the things Count Mippipopolous mentions as important to him satisfy physical cravings.

10. The count thinks Zizi has a good future, but he feels uncomfortable around him.

Suggested Essay Topics

1. Describe Count Mippipopolous. What things does he value? What do all those things have in common? How does he represent the "lost generation"?

2. Explain Brett's statement, "You haven't any values. You're dead, that's all." How does this describe Paris as a wasteland in Book I? How does this relate to the count? Jake? Herself?

The Sun Also Rises, Book II

Chapter 8

New Characters:

Bill Gorton: *Jake's fishing/bullfighting buddy; writer*

Madame Lecomte: *proprietor of Paris restaurant on Women's Club list*

Summary

As Book II begins, Jake says he does not see Brett again until she comes back from San Sebastian. He also mentions he does not see Robert during this time and Frances has left for England. Jake finds this break from Robert's company a good time to prepare for his trip to Spain at the end of June.

Bill Gorton comes to Paris with stories from travels—theater and prize fighting. He leaves for Vienna and Budapest; when he returns, he says he had a wonderful time. He loves Budapest, but his recollections of Vienna are vague because of his intoxication. One thing he remembers is that a black prize fighter knocked out a white fighter. When the black man started to make a speech, the white fighter went for him; the black knocked him out. When pandemonium broke out, the black man had to escape for his life.

Bill lent the black fighter a jacket. When he and Bill went back to get the prize money, promoters claimed the black owed them money. They claimed he had violated his contract by knocking out the white boy. He not only was not paid, but someone took his watch too.

When Bill and Jake go to dinner and drinks, they see Brett in a taxi. They stop for drinks, chat, and make plans to meet later when Mike arrives. They have dinner; then Bill and Jake walk along the river and enjoy the Paris night.

They go see Brett and her fiancé, Mike Campbell. Mike shows adoration for Brett, and they engage in conversation about her hat. Jake and Bill leave to go to a fight, and Mike and Brett are at the bar, drunk.

Analysis

Book II's initial setting is still in Paris but will eventually move to Spain where different values are established. This contrasts those seen so far in Paris by the lost generation's lack of traditional values. Bill first refers to values in his comment about stuffed animals. He says their purchase is a "Simple exchange of values. You give them money. They give you a stuffed dog."

This reference is similar to Brett's comment "You're dead, that's all" to the Count in the last chapter. It refers to the emptiness of the Paris crowd that has sold itself for money and pleasure. The taxidermist collects animals that were once alive just as Paris collects people who look okay but are dead to what is really important in life. Likewise, Brett has collected her trophies of men.

Brett has magic for men—now Mike and Bill. Mike, like Brett, is morally bankrupt, but he is also financially bankrupt. Mike's appearance in the novel shows the intense relationship Brett and Mike have, but it is based on sensual pleasures, and for Mike, often financial necessity.

Jake begins this book by hinting at not only Brett's role with Robert but also his relief Robert has been gone by saying he "enjoyed not having to play tennis." Although Brett's affair with Robert is foreshadowed by reference to their simultaneous absences, at this point Jake does not make the connection. Brett refers subtly, though, to her conquest of Robert in terms of San Sebastian. She says she "was a fool to go away" and says the trip (i.e., Robert) was "All right…Not frightfully amusing."

Brett refers to Paris as a haven and says, "One's an ass to leave Paris." Though she and Bill see Vienna with its bigotry and scandal, "Very much like Paris," she still appreciates all Paris has to offer. Brett has already established in previous chapters her feeling of social stratification when she sees the Count as "one of us."

Jake sees Paris as being corrupted by Americans. He and Bill go to a restaurant that has been crowded with Americans ever since being listed in the American Women's Club list. Jake does not go there often because there are "Too many compatriots." His aversion to the numbers of Americans in Paris who are violating places once enjoyable shows his disdain for their values.

Jake seems for the first time content with Paris as he and Bill walk along the Seine. This quiet reflection prepares the reader for their unity with nature in Spain as they appreciate the solace of the night. Bill does not even need a drink to appreciate it. It has not been spoiled by the values and presence of his compatriots.

The chapter is a prelude to their trip to Spain in two ways. First, solace and oneness with nature is relished in their night walk as it will be later on their fishing trip to Spain. Also, later values that will be developed are established by Bill Gorton's emphasis on prize fighters. The sense of fairness and right are the same values later compromised by Jake in regard to bullfighters.

Though Bill is unable to remember much about his trip, he can meticulously relate specific details about the story of prejudice and unfairness toward the black fighter. He observes there is "injustice everywhere." This begins to alert the reader to his value system. When the chapter ends, Jake and Bill are going to the fight, which possibly represents the constant fight mankind wages with his own values.

Study Questions

1. Who disappears at the same time as Brett?

2. What city has she gone to?

3. What city do Jake and Bill initially meet in?

4. Which city does Bill like?

5. What city does Bill encounter prejudice in?

6. What does Bill want Jake to buy?

7. What does Brett regret?

8. Who is Brett's fiance?

9. What does Mike dislike about Brett?

10. What does Mike tell about his financial situation?

Answers

1. Robert and Brett are both gone at the same time.

2. Brett has gone on a trip to San Sebastian.

3. Jake and Bill initially meet in Paris.

4. Bill enjoys Budapest.

5. While Bill is in Vienna, he encounters prejudice against a black man.

6. Bill wants Jake to buy an animal that has been stuffed by the taxidermist.

7. Brett regrets leaving Paris and going to San Sebastian.

8. Brett's fiancé is Mike Campbell.

9. While they are at the bar, Mike makes comments about disliking Brett's hat.

10. Mike tells he is bankrupt.

Suggested Essay Topics

1. Relate the incident with racial prejudice in Vienna. Why does Bill remember this so vividly? Why does Brett compare Vienna to Paris? How does she feel about this? Bill?

2. Contrast Mike and Bill. How do they each handle alcohol? What is the difference between their finances? What are their topics of conversation (i.e., prejudice in Vienna vs. Brett's hat)?

Chapter 9

New Characters:

Tourists from Montana (unnamed except for son Hubert): *on train to Spain*

Priest on Pilgrimage: *Catholic priest on train on pilgrimage to Rome*

Summary

After the prize fight, Jake receives a cable from Robert saying he will join them on their fishing trip. Jake cables him to meet them in Bayonne. Later when Jake sees Mike and Brett, they ask to go to Spain, too.

Mike leaves, and Jake and Brett are at the bar. When they are alone, Brett asks if Robert is going to Spain with them. She expresses concern and tells Jake she and Robert had been together in San Sebastian. Jake's sarcastic reaction shows his displeasure with the news. She tells Jake that on the trip, Robert had been dull. She also says she realizes seeing her in Spain with Mike will be hard on Robert.

They agree to let Robert decide about going. When Brett writes, though, Robert is excited about the idea. They make plans to meet in Pamplona.

Bill and Jake take the train where they sit with other Americans. They get sandwiches while awaiting their turn in the dining car and enjoy the passing scenery. When the train stops at Bayonne, Robert is awaiting them.

Analysis

One of the main occurrences in this chapter is the deepening of the breach between Robert and Jake. Jake had already begun to feel irritated with Robert; but after the revelation of his affair with Brett, Jake begins to feel animosity and disgust toward him. For example, at the station at Bayonne, for the first time Jake notices Robert is nearsighted. As it turns out, this is both literally and figuratively true where Brett is concerned.

Robert is infatuated with Brett, but she thinks he "gets a little dull." Because of his infatuation, Robert makes a foolish choice about going to Spain with Brett and Mike. He is unable to be objective while around Brett and will be hurt. Jake knows Robert is the type of commonplace man who could never satisfy Brett permanently, but he is still unable to handle the affair.

Regardless of that knowledge, the breach beginning between Robert and Jake is consummated by the physical consummation between Robert and Brett. By being able to satisfy Brett physically even for a time, Robert accomplishes what Jake will never be able to do for her. Jake's sarcastic "Congratulations" shows his disdain for their affair.

Jake's obvious hurt with the news continues with further sarcasm, a side of Jake the reader has not seen much before. When Brett says she "rather thought [the affair] would be good" for Robert, he responds she "might take up social service." Brett views her submission to Robert as a selfless act to aid Robert. It is, instead, another example of her lack of character. Her quest to satisfy physical and emotional needs precludes seeing what the relationship will ultimately do to Robert.

A contrast to the affair is the continuation of the feeling from the last chapter that Jake and Bill are at harmony with nature. They enjoy ripening grain and fields of poppies from the train window. They are on a train with Americans who are on a "pilgrimage to Rome." In essence, Jake, Bill, and Robert are on a pilgrimage toward Spain and reaffirming their values.

As they begin the quest for religious awakening and oneness on their fishing trip, Jake will serve as guide. Jake's religion is often mentioned but rarely is he connected with the established church. He is a man who has principles and appreciation of nature's handiworks, but he does not follow necessarily what the church says.

Although Jake is technically a Catholic, he is not a participant of the church now. Catholics can be seated in the dining car. Jake has to wait until later. Trying to buy off the conductor for earlier lunch does not work; money is not the answer to satisfy religious needs.

Study Questions

1. What kind of fight do Bill and Jake see at the beginning of the chapter?
2. Where does Jake cable Robert to meet them?
3. After Bayonne, where will they go on the bus?
4. What does Mike ask Jake's permission to do?
5. What is Mike waiting for before he goes with them?
6. Brett expresses concern about whose going on the trip?
7. What does Brett confide to Jake about her and Robert?
8. How does Jake react?
9. Why had Brett gone with Robert?
10. Where do Jake and Brett plan to meet?

Answers

1. At the beginning of the chapter, Robert and Jake are going to watch boxing.
2. Jake cables Robert to meet them in Bayonne.

3. After they leave Bayonne, the friends plan to go to Pamplona.

4. Mike wants to go with Jake and Bill to Spain.

5. Mike is waiting for his allowance to come.

6. Brett feels concern Robert will feel uncomfortable on the trip with her and Mike.

7. Brett tells Jake she and Robert had been together in San Sebastian.

8. Jake reacts to Brett's revelation by sarcastically commenting on the liaison.

9. Brett says she had gone with Robert because she thought the affair would be good for him.

10. Jake and Brett make plans to meet in Pamplona.

Suggested Essay Topics

1. How does Brett's revelation about San Sebastian affect Jake? Why had she gone? What does this tell about Brett? How does this drive a deeper wedge between Robert and Jake?

2. Describe the scenes on the train. How does the "pilgrimage to Rome" of the Catholics on the train parallel to the pilgrimage of Jake, Bill, and Robert? What are they looking for? What is the relationship of Jake to the Catholic church?

Chapters 10–11

New Characters:

Juanito Montoya: *Pamplona hotel owner; passionate bullfight enthusiast*

Basque: *peasant on bus*

Summary

The next morning Bill, Robert, and Jake buy fishing equipment. They hire a car and drive toward Pamplona where they wait at the border with armed guards. They see a man who is trying to cross the border waved back with guns. After they are cleared, they drive up into Spain. They climb into the mountains amid streams and fields of grain.

They drive to Pamplona past a grand cathedral and bullring to the Hotel Montoya. After they clean up, they have lunch, a typical Spanish meal with several courses. At lunch Robert at first seems awkward about his affair with Brett. After the subject is broached, though, he takes on a superior air of having inside information about her, which irritates Bill and Jake.

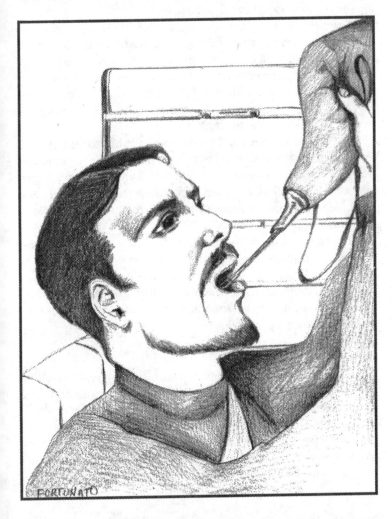

While they are awaiting dinner, each man goes to do individual activities. Jake makes sure his bullfight tickets are okay. Then he goes to the cathedral and prays for everyone he knows. Eventually his prayers go into secular thoughts, so he leaves.

At dinner, Robert's nervousness is obvious. He has shaved and cleaned up in anticipation of Brett's arrival. He leaves dinner early to go to the station in case Brett and Mike show up. Jake and Robert wait until the last person has gotten off the train, but Mike and Brett are not there. When they return, Jake receives a telegram saying they have stopped in San Sebastian.

The next morning Jake's disdain for Robert is deepened when Robert says he is not going fishing. He confides he is afraid Brett went to San Sebastian to meet him, so he stays to catch up with Mike and Brett. Jake explodes when he finds out Robert has confided his affair to Bill. Although Bill is irritated with him, too, he says he is glad Robert is staying because he and Jake will not have to deal with him on the fishing trip.

As Chapter 11 opens, Bill and Jake take the bus to Burguete for fishing. On the trip they share wine with peasants on the crowded bus. The bus stops a few places along the way to take on packages. One stop is at an inn, or posada, for passengers to rest and get a drink. After exchanging many drinks with Basques, the bus starts off again.

They meet a man on the bus who used to live in America. When they get to Burguete, they are met by a soldier who wants to know what is in their fishing case. They get a room; and when they come downstairs, the inn is so cold they can see their breaths. Wine comes with the room, so they get their money's worth. After supper they go to their room.

Analysis

Chapters 10 and 11 move Jake toward his destiny with his values. Religion is mentioned several times. Jake points out the monastery of Roncevalles. On the way to fish, they pass the church and schoolyard in Burguete. He also mentions his trip into Spain when a cathedral dominates the skyline. In Pamplona, he sees the church and bullring as dominant. All these relate to a time when the church was an integral part of the landscape. Those values are ones Jake missed in Paris.

In Pamplona, Jake goes into the church to pray, like a religious person. The church is dim, a good place for a sinner not to be confronted by his sins. However, though his prayers begin like the normal religious ritual, they become perverted when he prays for himself twice; then he prays he "would make a lot of money." His thoughts turn away from God to the Count, Jake's symbol of debauchery of the values he despises and that are so far from typical religion.

Robert is mentioned in a religious light but inappropriately, as is typical with Robert in social situations. First, Bill comments on Robert's being Jewish as a negative thing. Then, Robert notices the cathedral and says it is a "very good example of something or other," a comment that shows his lack of experience or refinement.

However, this comment also correlates to Jake's earlier observation that Robert developed his opinions through reading. Robert has textbook, not real-life, information about architecture just as he developed his sense of romance by reading, not doing. Jake, on the other hand, sees and appreciates Spanish cathedrals.

The affair between Robert and Brett is influenced by his books of gentlemen and lady-loves. Robert sees this as a grand affair, while Brett takes it casually. Robert acts nervous and awkward, but his having been one of her conquests has elevated Robert into a new social dimension.

Brett had gone to San Sebastian foolishly and selfishly so she did not have to go on her own, and Robert perceives the affair as something more. He ultimately overcomes his backwardness about the affair and likes being able to let people know, confidentially, there is something between him and Brett. However, instead of allowing him access to an inner circle, his relationship with Brett further alienates him from the group.

Jake and Bill both dislike Robert because of the affair. Bill dislikes his superiority and says "…As for this Cohn, he makes me sick." Jake's hatred escalates when he learns Robert has told Bill about the affair. Perhaps they see Robert's candor as a violation of his code. He has seen this affair as a chivalrous, noble thing like his readings. But part of a gentleman's obligation to his lady love is not to violate her confidence. He does not do that.

Jake's negative feelings also stem largely from his jealousy of Brett and Robert's San Sebastian fling. Jake tries to irritate Robert by mentioning Brett and Mike. At dinner Jake sees Robert's nervousness and does "not try to help him any." He goes with Robert to the train station "just to devil him." After receiving Brett's telegram, he does not let Robert see it just to further tease him. But Jake's feelings are more than mischief when he says, "I certainly did hate him."

As Bill and Jake go to Spain, they literally move up geographically as well in values. On the trip to Burguete, Basques are drinking wine as had been common in Paris. However, they are not drinking to excess for fun and are not people whose lives revolve around having fun. They are not idle rich but rather earthy, working people.

When Jake and Bill are at the border, the contrast is obvious. On the Spanish side, there are soldiers with uniforms carrying carbines. On the French side, guards are fat and sloppy. The Spanish soldiers are conscientious and challenge a pedestrian while the French do not. In Burguete, a soldier asks to see the fishing case to avoid smuggling and even asks for a fishing license. This emphasis on law and order is another contrast with the decadence of "anything goes" of France.

Study Questions

1. What does Jake buy before they leave?

2. Where do they hire the car to take them?

3. How do Spanish meals differ from American?

4. What do Robert and Bill bet on?

5. Why does Robert decide not to go fishing with Bill and Jake?

6. How does Bill react when he finds Robert actually did go with Brett to San Sebastian?

7. What kind of noise does the Basque on the bus imitate?

8. What type of apparel do the Basques wear?

9. How long had the man on the bus been in America?

10. What drink comes with the hotel room's price?

Answers

1. Before they leave on the trip, Jake buys tackle for fishing.

2. Jake, Bill, and Robert hire the car to take them to Pamplona.

3. In Spain, meals contain more courses.

4. Bill bets Brett and Mike will come to Pamplona that night, but Robert bets they will not.

5. Robert thinks he should go to Brett in case she had intended to meet him in San Sebastian.

6. Bill thinks Brett was foolish to go with Robert to San Sebastian.

7. On the bus, the Basque repeatedly imitates a Klaxon motor horn.

8. The Basques wear a black smock.

9. The man Bill and Jake meet on the bus had been in America 15 years.

10. Wine is included in the price of the room.

Suggested Essay Topics

1. Compare Bill and Jake's comments on surroundings with Cohn's for appropriateness. How is this indicative of the way Robert and Jake approach life? How does this impact the deterioration of Jake and Robert's relationship?

2. Contrast France and Spain. How does each represent a difference in values? What do the churches that are described have to do with those values? How does Jake's statement, "I only wish I felt religious and maybe I would the next time" fit this?

Chapter 12

New Characters:

Wilson Harris: *an Englishman staying in Burguete*

Bryan: *author Bill refers to*

Summary

Jake awakens the next morning and lets Bill sleep a while longer while he goes downstairs and to the stream to dig worms for bait. When he goes back to the inn, the proprietor is up. Jake orders coffee and a lunch for the fishing trip before going back to the room.

Bill is already awake. When they go to breakfast, Bill is light-hearted and singing. There is playful bantering, until Bill is afraid he has hurt Jake with a comment about impotence. They gather lunch and wine and go off to fish.

They go across open fields and streams. Finally, they reach the stream where they are to fish, put rods together, and begin. Jake puts the wine into the stream to keep it cold. Then he finds a place on the dam from which to fish. When he first puts his line in, he catches a fish. He takes it off and repeats the procedure until he has six fish. He wraps them and reads until Bill comes for lunch. While they are eating, Jake and Bill again begin a light-hearted conversation, likening their meal to a religious experience. They lie down for a nap beneath trees. While they are lying there, Bill asks about Jake and Brett's relationship. Jake is honest with him.

They nap for a while until the later afternoon. After they awaken, they pack up to leave. They begin the long walk back to Burguete but do not get there until after dark. They stay and enjoy fishing and swimming for five days, sometimes fishing with an Englishman named Harris.

Analysis

Chapter 12 is essential in moving toward Jake's experiences in Pamplona. He reminds the reader of his dissatisfaction with the lost generation's values through Bill's definition of expatriates who have emerged on the Paris scene. Bill defines these traits to Jake when he says if you are in that life, you can lose "touch with the soil…drink yourself to death…become obsessed by sex…spend all your time talking, not working."

Jake has been involved in the fast, nonproductive life of Paris, a wild life he has scorned. In Paris, drinks and food had been extravagant in a backdrop of clubs and drunkenness. These values are embodied in extravagant tastes of the Count who does whatever satisfies immediate cravings.

The fishing trip contrasts that lifestyle with the simplicity of lunch—wine, eggs, and chicken—in a backdrop of nature. Jake is so in tune with nature he drops his hook in the river, and trout nearly jump on it. He lacks unity and is even angered by things he scorns in Paris, such as the homosexual lifestyle.

Life in Burguete is slow-paced with an appreciation of nature resembling a religious experience. Jake and Bill walk through old trees, with sunlight pushing through. Similarly, traditional values are peeking through darkness for Jake. This experience becomes a pseudo-religious awakening for him.

While on the trip, Jake has noticed beautiful churches. This chapter goes further to say the woods are "God's first temples." As Bill and Jake sit to eat, their wine becomes as a communion. Bill says, "Our stay on earth is not for long. Let us rejoice and believe and give thanks." They mimic the prayer ritual by, "Let no man be ashamed to kneel here in the great out-of-doors." This kneeling refers to Catholicism, Jake's official religion.

Although Bill is being flip in saying, "Let us utilize the fowls of the air...the product of the vine," here lies the essence of Jake's values. There is a oneness with things natural and moral and ethical. This shows a desire for a time when life was simpler with an openness where friends can say, "I'm fonder of you than anybody on earth" rather than create facades like Brett and Jake have created for others to see.

In light of this, their prior conversation about irony and pity makes sense. As Bill reflects on irony and pity in life, he observes Cohn is pitiful because he is not at one with himself but rather chases a dream with Brett that will never materialize.

Jake says he has been in love with Brett off and on for a long time, but the irony and pity of his love is that, though he loves her intensely, he can never satisfy her in the way she wants to be satisfied. Jake's impotence is a strange irony. Even though he and Bill joke about the affliction, Jake's condition is how expatriate life is—impotent and unfulfilling.

The chapter ends with no word from Robert or Mike and Brett. They do not enter into the world where Jake and Bill have been re-born. Their bantering about the chicken or the egg coming first shows birth and rebirth of men. For these men, a rebirth has taken place.

Study Questions

1. What does Jake get at the stream while Bill is still asleep?

2. What words does Bill repeat and even sing to the tune of another song?

3. What kind of fish are they catching?

4. How do they keep their wine cold?

5. How many fish does Jake lay out at the dam?

6. What does Jake put between layers of fish?

7. What do they have for lunch?

8. How long do Bill and Jake stay in Burguete to fish?

9. Whom do they meet in Burguete who goes fishing with them?

10. What river do they fish in?

Answers

1. Jake gets worms for bait while Bill is asleep.

2. Bill repeats the words "irony and pity."

3. Bill and Jake are catching trout.

4. The men keep their wine cold by putting it in a cold stream.

5. Jake lays out six fish.

6. Jake separates layers of fish by placing ferns between them.

7. For lunch Jake and Bill have chicken and eggs.

8. Bill and Jake stay in Burguete for five days.

9. While they are in Burguete, Harris fishes with them.

10. The men fish in the Irati River.

Suggested Essay Topics

1. Comment on Bill's feelings about expatriates who lose "touch with the soil....drink yourself to death...become obsessed by sex...spend all your time talking, not working." How does this describe Jake or his friends? Jakes's attitude? Why is this good or bad?

2. Show how Bill and Jake's fishing trip is similar to a religious experience? How does the wine drinking resemble communion? How does Bill's observation "Our stay on earth is not long. Let us rejoice and believe and give thanks" relate? What does this have to do with the theme?

Chapter 13

Summary

One morning at breakfast in Burguete Jake receives a letter
from Michael saying they will all meet in Pamplona on Tuesday.
He apologizes for being late but says Brett had passed out, so they
had to take a few days to recuperate. Jake invites Harris to go with
them, but he declines so he can spend the rest of the time fishing.

Later when Bill and Jake are sitting on a bench in front of the
inn, a telegram comes from Robert. Jake and Bill are irritated with
its brevity, so they send a return telegram that is equally cryptic.
Afterward, they tour the local monastery with Harris and go to a
pub. Harris really enjoys their company. When he walks them to
the bus, he gives them envelopes containing fishing flies. They leave
for Pamplona.

When they arrive in Pamplona, people are already decorating
for the fiesta. At the hotel, Jake sees Montoya, the proprietor, who
tells him Mike, Brett, and Robert have arrived. Montoya says they
have gone to see pelota, a game resembling jai alai. Then he says
the running of the bulls will be tonight at 7:00.

Montoya respects Jake because of his passion, or *afición*, for
bullfighting. He treats Jake as if they have a secret between them.
The hotel is a meeting place of *aficiónados*, who receive honor from
people like Jake and Montoya. He has pictures of bullfighters on
the wall but only those whom he considers *aficiónados*. He keeps
others in a drawer or throws them away.

When Jake goes back to the room, Bill asks about the running
of the bulls. They find the others who are at a table in the street.
When they meet, Mike and Brett greet them warmly while Robert
merely acknowledges their arrival. Robert says he did not join Bill
and Jake to fish so he could bring Brett and Mike. Brett protests.

In the course of the discussion, they discuss Mike's past—his
war history and his bankruptcy. When he was invited to a dinner
by the Prince of Wales, he was asked to wear his medals. He borrowed some from a tailor. Later he gave them away to girls. The
tailor tried to get them back because they belonged to a military
man who had only sent them to the tailor to be cleaned. Mike did
not return them.

As the group walks down to see the bulls unloaded, Robert falls in beside Brett. People line the way to see the bulls. They watch as the first bull comes from the box into the corral with power. The bull goes first for steers, then charges a man. They watch the precision with which bulls move.

As a second bull comes out and gores a steer, Brett watches with fascination. The other steer is clipped but not killed. Then the two bulls and steer team up to make the new bull coming into the ring part of the group. Finally, with the last two bulls, they are all in submission as one herd.

After watching this, the crowd disperses, and they go for drinks at the cafe. As a discussion ensues about bulls and steers, Mike compares Robert to a steer. Conversation between Robert and Mike heats up, and Mike insults Robert repeatedly. Discussion turns to how Robert always follows Brett around like a steer.

Mike's insults of Robert continue. Robert stands as if to hit Mike but does not follow through with the threat. Mike says Robert was not invited to parties in San Sebastian because no one could stand to invite him. Finally, Bill feels sorry for Robert and leaves with him. Robert is obviously upset, and Jake and Brett are upset with Mike.

After Robert leaves, Brett concurs with Mike's feelings but disagrees with how he ridiculed Robert. Mike tells Jake how Robert came to San Sebastian to hang around Brett and had stared constantly at her. They ask Jake to tell Robert to change his ways or to get out of Pamplona.

When Jake goes to his room, he has a conversation with Montoya who expresses disappointment about the quality of bulls. When Jake sees Bill, he says Mike was terrible to Robert. As they get ready for dinner, they dread the unpleasantness that will follow the flare up between Mike and Robert. However, Mike acts as if nothing happened. After Robert is brought down, he finally warms up too. He keeps staring at Brett, however.

Analysis

As Chapter 13 opens, Jake, Bill, and Harris tour the monastery—the last bit of religion before going back to sinners transplanted from Paris. Harris realizes going back is "a pity" which reminds the reader of Bill's comments on pity earlier. This pseudo-religious experience prepares the reader for another strong aspect of Jake's inner values—that of an *aficiónado*.

Montoya respects Jake because he has a passionate awareness of bullfighting that most people, even some bullfighters, do not have. Like fishing, *afición* is a spiritual experience, almost religious. When Jake refers to his being accepted by Montoya's *aficiónado* friends, he says it was an "oral spiritual examination" to prove he was one of them. When they meet, both Montoya and his friends actually touch Jake, again similar to the religious ceremony of laying on of hands.

This passion is like a "special secret" understood by only a few. This feeling for bullfighting is the difference between an *aficiónado* and a fan. Montoya makes this clear in describing Bill as "not an *aficiónado* like" Jake. Montoya's *afición* is so powerful he knows the bulls are not top notch because of a feeling.

Montoya realizes the significance of *afición* in saying some things are excusable if one is an *aficiónado*. For example, some bullfighters may lose their nerve or behave badly. Also, some *aficiónados*, like Jake, may have undesirable friends. These things are forgivable if one is truly an *aficiónado*. *Afición* is an inner sanctuary.

Not only does Montoya recognize Jake's friends' undesirable traits, but Jake also shows them lacking inner qualities that make people worthwhile, especially in light of his fishing trip. Harris had given handmade fishing flies as medals to his newfound friends who had earned his respect. Mike, on the other hand, had given away borrowed medals to people who in no way deserved them. This shows a lack of character and untrustworthiness. Mike also says he went bankrupt because of friends and credit.

Mike lacks character in his treatment of Robert, too. He insults Robert in contrast to Bill who has a conscience. Although Bill does not like Robert at all, he feels Mike is wrong to talk to Robert as he does. He even defends Robert and shows his protectiveness by taking him away. Hemingway's treatment of Bill versus Mike shows strength of character of one with more traditional values versus new generation mores.

Mike's merciless insults of Robert are as vicious as Frances' in Paris. Again, Robert does nothing to defend himself but stand as if to hit Mike. Like a steer, he is basically impotent, to defend himself. When steers come into the ring, they cower at the sight of the bull. So does Robert when it actually comes to giving blows.

Jake and Robert are both like steers. Jake is nonproductive and physically impotent. Robert is also like a steer. Mike says, "They lead such a quiet life. They never say anything and they're always hanging about so." This reference is to how Robert has shadowed Brett.

Even Robert's comment, "It's no life being a steer" shows the irony of the bull comparison. Bulls have grace and power "just like a boxer." Ironically, though Robert was once a boxer to be admired, Jake was skeptical he ever actually did box. Robert could be a bull, but his lack of social skills makes him a steer.

The running of the bulls when a new one arrives in the pack shows territorial rites of old bulls. Mike's diatribe with Robert is a similar rite. There is dancing around until new bulls become part of the herd. Robert has not become one of them. Mike sees the difference between him and Robert when he says "Who has any breeding...except the bulls?" There is a social gap as well as a difference in attitudes between Robert and Mike.

Bulls gore steers as Mike does Robert, but steers cannot do anything because "They're trying to make friends." Robert told Jake earlier he has no friends, so he is unable to defend himself as one would with friends. Even after Mike has lambasted him so badly, Robert joins them as if they are friends. Bulls, like Mike, are only dangerous when they are alone or in small groups.

Brett, who has already shown her sexual priorities, admires the beauty of the bull. Unlike most women, Brett is fascinated with the goring of the steer. She had gored Robert, too, by her affair and later rejection of him. Although she protests Robert's goring by Mike, she is able to rationalize its necessity because Robert was so bad in San Sebastian.

Robert's infatuation with Brett only increases with her contempt for him. Her power is obvious even for women when the woman in the window calls to her girls who stare at Brett. Robert sees her power over him and calls her Circe because she turns men into swine. This comparison is interesting in light of the earlier references of the men to other animals—bulls and steers. Like victims of Circe, Robert has lost control with Brett.

By the end of the chapter the group has settled into a nice herd without the animosity of steers and bulls exerting territorial rights. Jake, however, is overcoming the feeling that something bad is going to happen. "It seemed they were all such nice people" he says at dinner. That, however, is an illusion.

Study Questions

1. Who gives Jake the letter from Michael?

2. Where are Bill and Jake meeting Brett and Michael?

3. From whom does Jake receive a telegram?

4. What does Harris give Bill and Jake as presents when they leave for Pamplona?

5. Why does Montoya respect Jake so much?

6. What are two things Mike says caused his bankruptcy?

7. To what does Jake compare the bull?

8. Who gets into an argument with Robert? Why?

9. How had Robert acted when he joined Brett and Mike in San Sebastian?

10. What pet name does Robert call Brett? Why?

Answers

1. Harris gives Jake the letter from Michael.

2. All of the friends will be meeting at the Hotel Montoya in Pamplona.

3. Jake receives a telegram from Robert Cohn telling of his arrival.

4. Harris gives parting gifts of fishing flies to Jake and Bill.

5. Montoya respects him because Jake has a passion, or *afición*, for bullfighting.

6. Mike says his bankruptcy was caused by friends and creditors.

7. Jake compares the bull to a boxer.

8. Mike gets into an argument with Robert because he is tired of Robert following Brett around everywhere.

9. In San Sebastian, Robert had followed Brett everywhere and stared at her constantly.

10. Robert calls Brett Circe because she turns men into swine.

Suggested Essay Topics

1. Discuss *afición*. How does Montoya treat *aficións* differently? How does this relate to Jake? Montoya? Bill?

2. What is the difference between bulls and steers? What does this conversation represent in the values and characters of the people of Hemingway's time? In Jake's group, who are bulls and who are steers?

3. Tell Mike's story of the medals. What does this demonstrate about his character? How is this incident representative of the "lost generation"?

Chapters 14–15

New Character:

Pedro Romero: Aficiónado; *19-year-old bullfighter; has an affair with Brett*

Summary

Jake, who is drunk, goes to his room and reads for a while until the room does not spin. He hears Brett and Robert come up and go to their separate rooms. Then he hears Mike and Brett talk and laugh. Jake is unable to sleep for thinking about them. Then he begins to philosophize about life, his friends, and morality. Finally, he gets up and reads again.

The next two days the friends are all subdued while the town readies for the fiesta, which is to last seven days. All in the group

have different activities. Jake and sometimes Bill watch the activities from the cafe or walk around the countryside in the afternoon. The last day before the fiesta, Brett and Jake go into the church. Although Robert follows and waits outside, everything is pleasant and casual.

In Chapter 15, Pamplona explodes with the fiesta. The first day of the fiesta, streets become crowded with people drinking and partying. Jake joins Robert and Bill at the cafe. As rockets explode to signal the beginning of the festival, masses of people converge on the square and cafe. All over, dancers and musicians celebrate.

First, comes a man playing a reed pipe with children following. Next come dancers, men dressed in workmen's blue smocks with red handkerchiefs around their necks. They are carrying a banner welcoming foreigners.

In the parade are dignitaries, whom the group cannot see because of the intense crowd. They start into church for services but decide not to go in because Brett is not allowed without a hat. The crowd forms a circle around Brett and begins to dance.

When the song ends, people take Brett into a wine shop and seat her on a wine cask. People are drinking and will not allow Jake to pay. Jake leaves to get a leather wine bottle. When he returns, Brett and Bill are in the back room. Jake fills the wineskins and goes to find them.

They are sitting on barrels surrounded by dancers. Mike is having hors d'oeuvres. Jake hands a wineskin around, and everyone takes a drink. Robert passes out, and they take him to the back room. He reappears two hours later. They finally all leave to clean up for dinner.

Jake plans to stay up to see the bulls run, but he goes to his room around 4 a. m. Since his room is locked, he sleeps in one of Robert's beds. Nothing awakens him until the exploding rockets signal the releasing of the bulls. In the thick crowd running in front of the bulls, one man falls and rolls into the gutter. When Robert comes in, he tells Jake that inside the ring, a bull had tossed six or eight people. Bill stops in; then they sleep until noon.

The next day the bullfight begins. Newcomers Brett, Mike, and Robert sit up high while veterans Bill and Jake sit ringside. When Bill cautions Robert about what to watch for, Robert says he may be bored. They warn Brett not to look at horses after the bull has gored them.

When Jake and Bill go to get wine and field glasses, Montoya introduces them to Pedro Romero, the newcomer and *aficiónado*, to bullfights. Romero is striking in his attire, manners, and good looks. They wish him luck and leave.

At the bullring, they are impressed with Romero's skill. Montoya is too and catches Jake's eye to nod his approval. One of the other two bullfighters is fair and the other passable, but Romero enchants the crowd.

After the bullfight, Jake and Bill leave and join the crowd inching its way to the fiesta. Dancers line the streets. As they are joined by Mike, Brett, and Robert, Mike comments on Romero's bullfighting prowess while Brett on his attractiveness. They turn their attention to taunting Robert about his comment that he may be bored and his getting ill at the sight of the horses' goring.

The next day, Romero steals the show. Brett, sitting between Jake and Mike, watches his body, movements, and form. Jake points out Romero's style is of the old school, which lends more credence to him as a bullfighter. The next day, Romero does not fight, and the following day there is just the fiesta.

Analysis

Chapters 14 and 15 are good companion chapters. Little happens plotwise in the first chapter, but the reader understands more about Jake's feelings. The second chapter contains a lot of plot events and moves the reader closer to Jake's final confrontation with himself and his conscience.

Jake is again presented as a man who is in love with a woman who will only cause him pain. Though he has been buddies with Brett and Mike, when he hears them together in their room, he is unable to accept their relationship as he does in the day. Jake realizes, "You have to be in love with a woman to have a basis of friendship," but sarcastically concedes women are "swell friends."

A twist to his feelings is he says he has not considered Brett's side of their relationship. Now, he realizes he has taken joy in Brett's friendship knowing his impotence makes it impossible for him to return pleasure. Knowing Brett is being satisfied by other men has hurt him. He thinks hurt is the, "Presentation of the bill. The bill always came." This concept was first introduced by Brett's earlier comment about always paying for actions.

Since the plot is moving toward Jake's violation of his values, understanding them is important. Jake feels knowing what "it" is—discovering what one values—determines how people should live. He says "it" is not about understanding all details but rather knowing how to be comfortable with "it." To Jake, philosophizing is in itself "bilge" because it is concerned with why, not how. He has lived for superficial things that could be purchased and thought "Enjoying living was learning to get your money's worth." He realizes some things are not easily purchased.

Jake has demonstrated a sense of morality with other people's actions, but now he defines it for himself. Morality is shown by "things that made you disgusted afterward." For example, Jake realizes he feels uncomfortable with Mike's cruelty to Robert but not

HURRAY FOR WINE! HURRAY FOR FOREIGNERS!

FORTUNATO

because he feels sorry for him. He likes to see Cohn hurt by Mike, but he regrets his pleasure afterward because it shows character flaws. Therefore, when Jake enjoys Robert's hurt or later sets up Brett with Romero, he shows his immorality by acting on things that later cause regrets.

Part of Robert's downfall is his trying to fit in with a group whose values are different from his. He decides to live life and fall in love, but he is doing so outside his value system from examples in books, not life. He alienates Bill, who sees even his faith as negative, by his superior attitude. He alienates Mike and Brett by his infatuation for Brett that cannot be reciprocated. He alienates Jake by both his affair and later attitude.

His comment about being bored shows both his lack of understanding about the sport and his not being in his element. Robert has been good at many sports, but with bullfighting, he says he likes the show but does not like the sport. Robert has been a sports participant, not a spectator. This is also his attitude toward the group. He tries to become involved in their world because they represent something glittering and desirable. But the sport in which they participate is more than Robert's values can comprehend.

Other differences between the rest of the group and Robert are also apparent. He says he wishes horses did not have to be hurt because he, unlike Mike, is sensitive to the pain of others, even a horse. Before the fiesta when the others are spending time sleeping late or taking walks, Robert is learning Spanish or getting shaved. Jake says Robert never gets drunk, but when he does emulate their behavior by doing so, he is unable to cope and passes out.

Robert's difference in values from the group is also shown in comments about Brett. In the last chapter, Robert compares Brett negatively to Circe. He now sees her infatuation with the horses' demise as sadistic. Though she is cautioned not to watch horses die, she is fascinated and has an almost orgasmic reaction when, after the fight, she is "limp as a rag." Mike, unlike Robert, sees her as "just a lovely, healthy wench."

Brett seems a paradox who on one hand wants to hear Jake's confession, and on the other symbolizes the debauchery Jake detests. She is constantly the center of attention but often because of wild things as with the dance. She never really fits into a religious setting, though, as when she keeps Jake from worshipping because she has no hat.

The true focus of this reading, however, is on the character of Romero. His character is a pseudo-priest, the epitome of the intense sport that is honored by this celebration lasting seven days, a religious number. He is straight, direct, intense, clear, pure, and honest.

When Romero is introduced to Jake, he is in a room with "a monastic partition" and is attended by men who wait on his needs. Romero does not have to develop *afición* but is a natural, and "The others can't ever learn what he was born with." Immediately Jake and Montero sense, "This was a real one," in essence, a Christ figure.

Later, they see Romero has classic style and fights with grace and flare. But Romero also symbolizes Hemingway's code for living and writing. A person does not glide through life without experiencing or taking chances but rather he should, "let the horns pass...close each time." Accosting life like Jake rather than reading about it like Robert is Hemingway's code. Jake recognizes that knowing how to live is more important than the "bilge" of asking why things are because one should be more concerned with participating than with spectating. Jake's status as an *afciónado* is part of this code.

Before the fiesta the atmosphere was "fresh and cool...we felt good and...healthy and...friendly...You could not be upset." The fiesta with its ritual dancing and partying makes "Everything...quite unreal finally and...as though nothing could have any consequences." This creates the setting for Brett's affair with Romero and Jake's role in the violation.

Study Questions

1. Whom does Jake think he has not been considerate of?

2. How does Jake categorize his various friends' abilities to hold alcohol?

3. How does Robert spend his time before the fiesta?

4. What is written on the banner being carried into the fiesta?

5. How long is the fiesta?

6. Whom do the dancers put into the center of the group as an image to dance around?

7. How much does Jake pay for the wineskins?

8. Who passes out from drinking too much?

9. Before it starts, what is Robert afraid will happen during the bullfight?

10. How old is Romero?

Answers

1. Jake thinks he has not been considering Brett's feelings.

2. Jake feels Mike is a bad drunk; Brett and Bill are good drinkers; Cohn never gets drunk.

3. Before the fiesta, Robert studies Spanish or gets a shave.

4. The banner reads, "Hurray for Wine! Hurray for the foreigners!"

5. The Pamplona fiesta lasts seven days.

6. The dancers place Brett into the center of their group and dance around her.

7. Jake pays eight pesetas for two wineskins.

8. Robert passes out from drinking too much.

9. Robert is afraid he may be bored during the bullfight.

10. Romero is 19 years old.

Suggested Essay Topics

1. Explain Jake's statement, "Enjoying living was learning to get your money's worth and knowing when you had it." What is "it"? Why is Jake more interested in how to live rather than why? Where does Jake's relationship with Robert fit into this?

2. Show Romero as a Christ figure. What are the circumstances when the reader first sees him? Explain the quote, "The others can't ever learn what he was born with." How does this fit the religious reference?

Chapter 16

New Characters:

Edna: *Bill's friend from Biarritz who parties in Pamplona*

Marcial Lalanda: *a fading bullfighter*

Don Manuel Orquito: *the fireworks king*

Raphael: *bullfight critic with Romero*

Algabeno: *bullfighter hurt in Madrid*

Summary

The next morning rain and fog drive the fiesta inside. When Jake goes to his room, Montoya comes to see him. He tells Jake that the American ambassador has sent for Romero and Lalanda to join him for coffee. Montoya expresses concern that, although this action would be good for Lalanda, attention may spoil Romero. Jake suggests Montoya does not give him the message.

After Montoya leaves, Jake goes for a walk and to dinner. His friends have been drinking for a while, so Jake feels out of place. Romero, who is at the next table, invites him to his table. Jake meets Romero's friend, a bullfight critic. They talk for a while about Romero's career and tomorrow's fight.

As they are talking, Brett calls from the other table. She insists on being introduced and has obviously not taken her eyes off Romero. They move to another table and Brett sits by Romero. Mike is drunk and saying things about Brett. After toasts, Romero leaves. Then Mike and Robert again have words about his hanging around Brett. Mike and Robert nearly come to blows until Jake intervenes.

Jake and Mike leave. As they are standing in the square, Brett and Bill join them. They watch fireworks that do not dissipate but rather fall to the sidewalk. They go back into the cafe for a drink, but it is too crowded. They are joined by Bill's friend Edna and finally go to a bar to drink. Mike begins to flirt with her.

When people filter away, Brett and Jake are left with Robert hanging around. Brett rudely tells him to leave so she can talk to Jake. They both express hatred and disgust for Robert. As they take off from the bar, they notice Robert has been outside watching

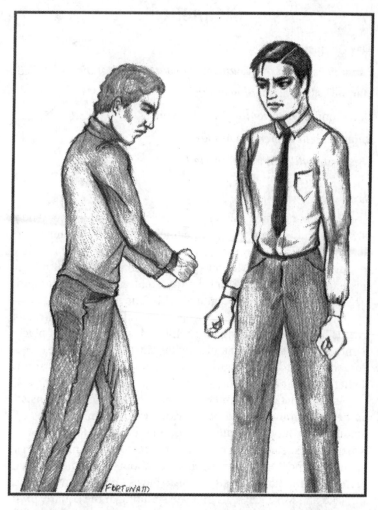

FORTUNATO

them. They walk, then sit silently in the moonlight. Brett confides
to Jake she has fallen in love with Romero. She asks Jake to arrange
the affair.

They find him in the cafe. Brett is nervous and says she has
never felt this insecure before. Romero joins them. As they are sitting, Brett takes his hand to tell his fortune. Jake signals to Romero
this is okay, and Jake makes an excuse to leave. When he checks
the cafe 20 minutes later, they are gone.

Analysis

The rain at the beginning of Chapter 16 is a Hemingway signal of impending disaster. This chapter covers several occurrences, but it basically focuses on one event—Brett's affair with Romero and Jake's role in it.

As Brett and Jake are walking, Brett is worked up. She first asks Jake if he loves her. She then says she is "a goner." Her hands are trembling, and she tells Jake she has lost self-respect. She has always done whatever she wanted to do, but this is different from her other conquests. When she begins to flirt with Romero, she loses all nervousness, though. She is in familiar territory.

Jake also realizes potential consequences of the affair to Romero as a bullfighter. At the beginning of the chapter, Jake sees the importance of not spoiling Romero by suggesting Montoya keep Romero from the American ambassador. However, when Brett asks for his help, he does so although she poses a greater threat.

This endangers Jake's position with other *aficiónados*. Montero sees Romero drinking cognac and sitting with a woman "with bare shoulders" and "did not even nod" at Jake. Later after Jake has actually gotten them together, "The hard-eyed people at the bullfighter table watched me go. It was not pleasant." Jake is violating their trust and acceptance of him.

Jake is also violating himself. Earlier he tells Brett if he had had the affair with her instead of Robert, he would "be as big an ass as Cohn," because of Brett's lackadaisical attitude. Although he loves Brett, he makes it possible for her to be Romero's lover, which leads to Robert's later charge that Jake is a pimp.

Brett's affair with Romero is a stark contrast with her affair with Robert. For Brett, she is as nervous as a girl about Romero. Her affair with Robert, though, "didn't mean anything." She not only does not sympathize with his love but is rude to Robert. She says she hates Robert's "damned suffering."

Unlike Romero, Robert is a loser and sufferer—a wimp. Mike recognizes Robert's difference when he asks, "Do you think you belong…People who are out to have a good time." Robert's moment of grandeur comes as a result of his affair with Brett. Although Mike is vicious to him, Robert enjoys being insulted because it "was his affair with his lady of title" as his books have often shown him.

He shadows Brett as a stalker and is not dissuaded even by her rudeness.

Romero has a sense of grandeur and position independent of Brett. He is concerned with appearances and says, "It would be very bad, a torero who speaks English." He knows his significance, and Brett responds to the take-charge attitude. Robert tries to be assertive and make a grand gesture when he stands as if "to do battle

FORTUNATO

for his lady love." Here, though, is his social impotence—he does not fight.

Study Questions

1. Why doesn't Montoya want Romero to have coffee with the ambassador?

2. What does Bill keep doing to Mike?

3. Where did Romero learn English?

4. What does Jake lie to Romero about?

5. What does the critic compare the bulls' horns to?

6. Who nearly come to blows?

7. Where is Robert when Brett and Jake come out of the bar?

8. Whom has Brett fallen for?

9. While they are sitting at the table, what does Brett tell Romero she will do for him?

10. Under what pretense does Jake leave Brett and Romero?

Answers

1. Montoya is afraid if Romero has coffee with the ambassador, the attention will spoil Romero.

2. As a joke, Bill keeps getting men to shine Mike's boots.

3. Romero had learned English in Gibraltar.

4. Jake lies when he tells Romero he saw him fight in Madrid.

5. The critic with Romero compares the bull's horns to bananas.

6. During the course of the conversation, Mike and Robert nearly come to blows.

7. Brett and Jake know Robert has been waiting for her because he walks out from under the arcade.

8. Brett has fallen in love with Romero.

9. While they are sitting at the table, Brett says she can tell Romero's fortune.

10. Jake lets Brett and Romero be alone by saying he has to go find their friends.

Suggested Essay Topics

1. Describe the setting up of Brett and Romero's affair. What is the significance of it? Tell why Jake's role in the affair violated his code. Discuss Robert's charge that Jake is a "pimp."

2. Explain why Montoya wants to protect Romero. How does he do that? How does Jake react to the invitation from the American ambassador? How does his involvement with Brett and Pedro contradict this? How does Montoya react?

Chapter 17

New Characters:

Charlie Blackman: *Edna's friend from Chicago; just mentioned in the story*

Vincente Girones: *a 28-year-old man who is gored and killed by a bull*

Summary

Jake finds Mike, Bill, and Edna outside a bar. They tell him they were thrown out when they got really drunk. They were in a fight with Englishmen and got rowdy.

They go to a cafe for a drink. Robert comes and asks where Brett is. Jake tries to put him off, but Robert persists. He panics when Jake refuses to tell him; then Mike says Brett has gone off with Romero. Robert gets angry and calls Jake a pimp. Jake swings at Robert, who ducks before hitting Jake. He tries to get up but Robert hits him two more times. He then hits Mike and leaves.

After he is gone, Mike and Edna rehash what happened. Jake is still dazed and decides to walk it off. Even on familiar terrain, he seems to experience the night for the first time.

When Jake stumbles back to the hotel, Bill tells him Robert is upset and wants to see him. At first Jake refuses. When he agrees, he goes to the room and finds Robert crying. Robert begs his for-

giveness and says he was crazy. He says he has not been able to
stand it. Brett has treated him as a stranger and now has gone off
with Romero. Robert vows to leave in the morning.

Jake leaves Robert's room and goes to take a bath. Then he
sleeps. After Jake awakens, he goes out to watch the bulls running
into the ring. The crowd is so thick, Jake is pushed against the wall.
Some people are unable to get into the ring before the bulls, and
Jake witnesses one man getting gored. Later the same bull is killed
by Romero, who gives its ear to Brett. Jake can only hear by the
crowd's reaction how many other people have been hit or had close
calls to the bulls.

When Jake goes back to his room, Mike and Bill come in and
comment on his wounds from Robert. They tell Jake what happened inside the ring. They say after Robert hit them, he found
Brett in Romero's room and nearly killed him. Even though Robert
had kept knocking him down, Romero had refused to stay down.
After Brett lambasted him, Robert broke out crying and apologized.
When Robert tried to shake Romero's hand, Romero refused. Robert told Romero he would not hit him again, so Romero hit Robert
as hard as he could.

Mike says part of the problem is because Brett chooses the
wrong type of man. Then he relates how unhappily Brett had been
married to Lord Ashley. Mike rings for the maid to bring him more
beer before he goes to his room. Bill and Jake are going to nap too.

Analysis

Chapter 17 focuses on Robert's reaction to Brett's affair. Brett
has used Robert, and now she hurts him by insulting him. Robert
had hoped his affair with Brett would fill the void in his unfulfilled
life. Robert's affair was supposed to be his elusive love and excite-
ment for him. Instead, it takes its toll. He has lost Jake, his only
friend, and he has lost any hope for love from Brett.

Jake has perceived Robert as enjoying Mike's abuse because it
calls attention to his trophy of having had Brett. Instead of being
the consummate relationship, now Robert says, "Everything's gone.
Everything." He is able to beat his competitors with his fists, but
Romero really wins because he does not give up. Even in victory,
Brett would never be his; she is repulsed by him. Robert has been

FORTUNATO

terribly abused by Brett, Mike, and Jake, but instead of knowing he is justified by his indignation, he apologizes to them.

Throughout preceding chapters, whenever Robert wants to present a threat, he stands and makes fists. He has power but only follows through when Brett is at stake. When he does, Romero breaks what little spirit Robert has by refusing to quit. When Robert will not defend himself, Romero hits him. In essence, Romero "ruined Cohn...Cohn will [never] want to knock people about again." He not only annihilated Robert's boxing prowess but also his hopes of having true love.

Through these events, Robert and Jake's relationship finally erupts. Robert has never perceived Jake as a threat for Brett. When Jake returns without her, he says, "She was with you." Jake is unable to beat Robert in boxing or in satisfying Brett. However, he does defeat him by following through with the threat to fight and by giving her to Romero. Through Romero, Jake becomes a vicarious threat.

On the other hand, by hurting Robert, Jake also hurts himself. The word "pimp" bothers Jake because of its truth. He has sold not only Brett but himself and his *aficiónado* values. After Robert hits him, he suddenly sees truth as one might in a religious experience and sees life as he never has before. Then when he takes a bath, he immerses in a baptism of water and cleanses himself of his sins. Similarly, Robert seeks absolution from Jake as he would a priest.

Jake's telling of the story becomes confusing after this. For the only time in the novel, Jake does not use chronological order. Before he tells of the last day of the fiesta, he tells of Vincente, who is killed by the bull. This happens "all for sport" instead of for some great cause. He tells how ultimately the bull is killed by Romero. Robert is killed by Brett who is eventually killed by Romero.

Jake also sets the stage for Brett's ultimate fate. Brett is presented as a survivor. Although Mike says she should know sleeping with a bullfighter and Jew would end badly, he also tells how she has made poor choices even with men who were aristocratic. When she was married to Lord Ashley, he would not sleep in a bed. He threatened to kill Brett and often slept with a loaded gun.

Brett's true love was lost in the war, but now she has another chance. She has fallen for someone with depth of character unlike others she has had in the past. It seems an appropriate ending that Brett is given the prize of the bull's left ear by Romero. She puts it in Jake's handkerchief and leaves it with cigarette stubs in a drawer of the table in the Hotel Montoya. Thus, though all the things in that drawer have little intrinsic worth, they represent Brett's life experiences and her leaving them shows a lack of appreciation for them.

Study Questions

1. Who is Bill's friend?
2. Why had they been thrown out of the bar?
3. Why does Robert panic when he sees Jake?
4. What does Robert call Jake?
5. Who swings at Robert in the cafe?
6. Who wants to see Jake when he gets to the hotel?
7. How does Robert rationalize his behavior to Jake?
8. Whom does the bull kill?
9. What literary technique does Hemingway use to make the story of the bull stand out from the rest of the novel?
10. How many people are taken to the infirmary because of the bulls?

Answers

1. Bill's friend in the reading is Edna.
2. Bill, Edna, and Mike are thrown out of a bar because they have been fighting with some Englishmen.
3. Robert panics at seeing Jake because Brett is no longer with him.
4. When Robert finds out Jake has fixed up Brett and Romero, he calls Jake a "pimp."
5. Jake swings at Robert in the cafe.
6. Robert says he wants to speak to Jake.
7. Robert says he has acted badly because he is crazy about Brett, and she has treated him badly ever since San Sebastian.
8. The bull kills Vincente Girones, a man who is in town to see the bullfights.
9. In order to make the story of the bull distinct from the rest of the novel, Jake tells the story out of chronological sequence.
10. About 20 people are taken to the infirmary because of the bulls.

Suggested Essay Topics

1. Describe Robert's fights for Brett. How does this relate to Robert's experiencing life through books? Why is Robert the loser though he badly beat Jake? Romero?

2. Describe Jake's awakening after Robert calls him a "pimp" and hits him. Why is the statement the truth? How does his walk show renewed sensations about life? What does the bath represent?

3. Explain the quote, "All for sport. All for pleasure." How does this relate to bullfighting? Relationships? The "lost generation"? Jake?

Chapter 18

New Character:

Belmonte: *a retired bullfighter who returned to the ring*

Summary

On the last day of the fiesta, Brett stops by, gets a beer, and asks if Robert has gone. She asks Jake how he feels. She tells him Robert has hurt Romero badly. Mike, who is drinking, has been silent. He starts ridiculing Brett for her affairs with Romero and Robert. Brett asks Jake to take a walk. She is radiant and shows adoration and concern for Romero. She also says his people disapprove of her. They stop in a church to say prayers for Romero.

When they get back to the hotel, she joins Romero in his room for lunch. Jake goes to Mike's room and finds him trying to sleep off his drunkenness. Bill and Jake eat at a restaurant and talk little. Brett joins them when they are finished.

The three of them go to the bullring and sit together. For this final day, the president is in attendance and lots of pomp and circumstance accompanies it. When the matadors come into the ring, Romero is in the center. His hat is low to cover bruises from Robert. The matadors go into the ring and bow in front of the president's box. Then, Romero hands his gold-brocade cape to his sword handler who hands it to Brett.

Belmonte is first. His fight is without much drama, and the

crowd is actively against him. He is not interested in Marcial but rather in Romero whose popularity has hurt his coming out of retirement. Romero does his fighting the way Belmonte cannot anymore. Marcial performs next.

Romero fights next. He works perfectly despite the bull's poor vision and the injury he suffered from Robert's beating. The crowd wants another bull, but Pedro fights this one. Romero lets the bull pass close by, and it is very dangerous. But the crowd feels cheated

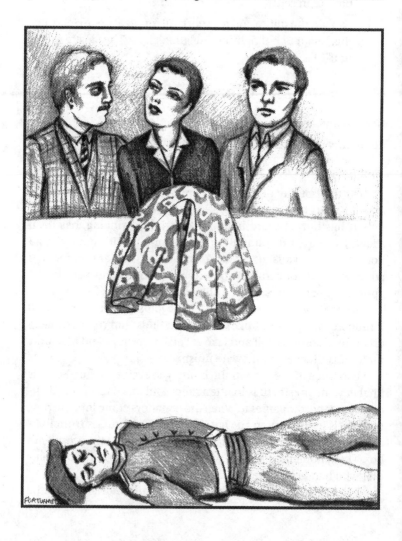

and is against Romero for this fight. Marcial is next and has the crowd ecstatic.

Romero's last bull is the one that killed Vincente in the morning. It is a good bull that works easily and charges well. Although Romero works smoothly and efficiently, when he begins to kill it, the crowd wants him to continue. He does. When he finally kills the bull, Romero gives the ear to Brett. The crowd is so enthralled with Romero they mob him and lift him to their shoulders.

After the bullfight, the group goes back to the hotel to eat and drink. Bill expresses interest in how Robert is doing and where he will go. Jake says he does not care, but he works hard to get drunk to feel better. Jake goes to his room feeling drunker than he ever has. He sticks his head in Brett's room. Mike tells him Brett has gone off with Romero. Jake lies down but cannot sleep. When he joins Mike and Bill, the dining room seems vacant.

Analysis

Chapter 18, not told in true chronological order, is the end of the fiesta and focuses on the last bullfighting day. Jake contrasts the three bullfighters' styles.

First, the oldest, and at one time most respected, is Belmonte. He is a bullfighter of great renown who has come out of retirement but cannot live up to his own reputation. He is sick now and picks and chooses easier bulls. Now he occasionally has great moves in the ring, but even Belmonte does not consider them of any value because he has chosen bulls in advance.

Marcial is a fighter with whom Belmonte feels no competition. Though he is the one Belmonte came out of retirement for, he knows Marcial is no competitor because he only goes through the motions and does not fight with sincerity of *aficiónados*. Though Marcial has a good day and the crowd is with him, he is not Belmonte's rival. Belmonte watches Romero, not Marcial.

Belmonte's performance is an "imitation of himself" and Marcial's is an "imitation of Belmonte," but Romero is pure bullfighting. Romero's natural flair has fans on his side. His style is so intense he has spoiled Belmonte's return to the ring.

Romero moves like the old style fighters, keeping the bull close to his body, "rocking the bull to sleep." He uses showmanship and observes rituals associated with the fight. For example, he notes

Brett should not spread the cape out but should keep it folded in her lap. He also strives to please the crowd in the process. When the bull is finished, he continues with the show as the fans wish.

Romero loves bullfighting, bulls, and Brett. He is a true leader. At the beginning of the fights, Romero is standing in the center with the other two bullfighters on either side, a sort of Christ figure. Like Christ, he is badly bruised from his fight with Robert, but it "had not touched his spirit."

Religious references also relate to Brett, a sort of Mary Magdalene figure. Romero's people are angry about Brett, a woman of some dubious character. Christ's followers also question the wisdom of his associating with a prostitute. Like Magdalene, Brett has had a metamorphosis. She is in love. She sees a bright day because she is a changed woman. She is used to being stared at, but she cannot stand it now. Later she even makes an unselfish decision about Romero's career.

Unlike Magdalene, though, Brett's conversion is incomplete. She asks Jake to go to San Fermin to pray for Romero but soon realizes she is "damned bad for a religious atmosphere." She says church "never does me any good" and she has never gotten anything she prayed for. Her comment she has the "wrong type of face" shows her lack of understanding that conversion is within rather than on the outside.

Jake, on the other hand, says he has gotten answers to his prayers. He says he is "pretty religious." However, by his role in the affair, he has violated both his values and dignity. To forget them, he "began to feel drunk but...did not feel any better." He also feels guilt when Montoya bows to him and Brett but does not smile. Jake's conscience will be appeased not by getting "tight," but by true forgiveness of his spirit. Later he will seek that through his trip.

The end of Book II leaves not only Brett and Jake with these dilemmas but also Mike. He is bankrupt—financially, morally, spiritually, and behaviorally. His experiences have left him with nothing from the days in Pamplona. Mike has even lost Brett. He tells Jake, Brett has "gone off with the bull-fighter chap." The other two characters have had experiences that have made them richer people. Mike's lack of values, on the other hand, has created a greater void for him.

Study Questions

1. At the beginning of the chapter, who has left?

2. Who is in bad shape from Robert's beating?

3. What does Brett want to do in San Fermin?

4. What is the nationality of the maitre d' at the hotel?

5. What is in the baskets carried by the sword handlers and bull-ring servants?

6. What official is attending the final fight?

7. What is wrong with Romero's first bull?

8. To whom does Romero give the bull's ear?

9. What does Jake say Robert will do now?

10. Where is Brett?

Answers

1. Robert leaves after his altercation with the others about Brett.

2. Romero has been badly beaten by Robert.

3. When she and Jake are in San Fermin, Brett prays for Romero.

4. The hotel maitre d' is German.

5. The sword handlers' baskets are holding fighting capes and muletas.

6. The president is watching the bullfights on the last day of the fiesta.

7. Romero's first bull presents a challenge because it cannot see well.

8. After Romero has killed the bull, he cuts off the ear and gives it to Brett.

9. Jake assumes that, now that Robert has accepted his loss of Brett, he will go back to Frances.

10. Brett has left Pamplona with Romero.

Suggested Essay Topics

1. Describe the ceremony before and during the final bullfight. Why does Romero wait to kill the bull? What are examples of the tradition involved? Compare Romero's final fight with his fight with Robert.

2. Compare and contrast the three bullfighters. Why does Romero's attention to the old style make him more skillful? Why does Belmonte think "Pedro had the greatness"? Do their styles suggest other characters in the novel?

The Sun Also Rises, Book III

Chapter 19

New Character:

Maid: *at the Hotel Montana in Spain*

Summary

As Book III opens, the fiesta is over. The town is taking down posters and traces of what was. Bill tells Jake he is going back to Paris, but Jake says he will be going to San Sebastian. They pay their bill; then Mike, Bill, and Jake drive into the country.

They stop in Biarritz to have a drink. They keep rolling dice for drinks, and Mike loses. Finally, he says he cannot buy anymore because he is out of money. Mike bemoans his financial woes since his allowance has not come yet. They drive around for a while. Then Mike stays in Saint Jean because he can stay there on credit.

After they part, Jake goes to Bayonne and stays one night. He feels good to be in France again but does not want to go to Paris with Bill. Jake has dinner and enjoys food and wine. The waiter gets offended by Jake's wanting the flowers removed but is appeased by his generous tip.

Jake then boards a train for San Sebastian. He spends his time swimming and being lazy. Later when he is having dinner, riders in a bicycle race stop for the night in San Sebastian. Racers seem lax in their racing.

The next day, Jake does more of the same. After three days he receives two cables from Brett; she is at the Hotel Montanya in Madrid and needs help. Jake gets a berth on the Sud Express and travels during the night to arrive in Madrid.

When Jake arrives, the maid at the hotel tells Jake he may see Brett if she wishes. He has his bags brought in. When the maid returns saying he may go up, Jake goes to Brett's room. She is in bed and says she made Romero leave her. She realizes she is bad for him.

She says she does not want to talk about it but begins anyway. Romero is ashamed of her. When she starts to leave, he offers her money, but she cannot take it. She says he wants to marry her to try to possess her. She left him because it is best for him.

Jake thinks Brett is looking for a cigarette but sees she is actually crying. She decides to go back to Mike. When they check out of the hotel, they find the bill has been paid. They sit in the hotel bar to have a drink. Brett talks about hers and Romero's age difference. During dinner, Brett cannot stop talking about Romero.

They decide to take a ride to see Madrid. They get in the taxi and Brett moves closer to him. As the story ends, she bemoans she and Jake could have been good together. Jake agrees.

Analysis

As this chapter opens, Jake is trying to get away from the fast life of the fiesta. He realizes he "was through with fiestas for a while." His sin is accentuated when Montoya does not come near Bill and Jake as they check out. He knows he must find inner peace.

Initially, he goes back to France but not to the old, wild life in Paris. He feels comfortable in France because he can make friends there just by tipping well since "Everything is on such a clear financial basis." Jake feels a degree of comfort in this simplicity. He knows "if they remembered me their friendship would be loyal." Jake has been too long with those who measure friendship by money.

Before the car leaves, Jake rubs the rod case with dust. "It seemed the last thing that connected me with Spain and the fiesta." Somehow Jake must make a final break, though. In Bayonne he stays in the same room as he had with Bill, but that trip seems "a very long time ago," and he is unable to recapture that solace. He has a new awareness of himself and must find peace. Although he says he feels foolish to be going back into Spain, he travels there to cleanse himself.

Jake goes to San Sebastian, ironically where Robert and Brett had the affair. There, he has no deadlines to meet or parties to attend. Like on the fishing trip, he becomes at one with himself. He swims, reads, and relaxes.

FORTUNATO

This spiritual rejuvenation is necessary for his next meeting with Brett. When he watches the bicycle riders, he realizes they "do not take the race seriously except among themselves" and it "did not make much difference who won." Jake's friends are in a bicycle race while he is a bullfighter. Jake wants to live a life where it does make a difference.

By the time he receives Brett's cables, he is able to put things into perspective. "Send a girl off with one man. Introduce her to another to go off with him. Now go and bring her back. And sign the wire with love." At this point, he is able to see Brett and his involvement objectively. He not only has come to terms with his actions but also has purged Brett from his system.

Brett's character now seems to have some redeeming qualities. She makes decisions about her future with a man based on his needs rather than her own. Brett would have liked to live with Romero, but she knows that would have been bad for him because Romero is really only interested in bullfighting. Brett feels good to do something with another person's interests in mind. "It's sort of what we have instead of God," she muses.

Unlike other relationships, she does not hurt Romero. With Mike, Jake, and Robert, she did not worry about how they felt in their love for her. She is now not only generous to Romero's feelings, she is generous with Mike. She gives most of her money to Mike for the bill to Montoya.

Brett has had to face truths about herself. She is not a typical woman and would be a terrible mother. She has also seen her mortality because no one has ever been ashamed of her as Romero was of her hair and age. Romero wants to marry her but for the wrong reasons. He wants to possess her and change her to be more womanly.

When Jake finds out she has left Romero, he asks Brett, "Why didn't you keep him," like Romero was one or her possessions. At this point, however, she realizes a decent man like Romero is too good for her. Mike is her "sort of thing. He's so damned nice and he's so awful." She realizes even Jake is different when she comments he does not have to get drunk like the others. Brett has had an awakening, too.

Jake knows nothing will ever materialize for him and Brett. He says Madrid is where all rails finish. "They don't go anywhere" nor does his relationship with Brett. It ends as their relationship in the book had begun. They are riding in a taxi just like in Paris, but this time Brett is close to Jake instead of pushing him away. They have come full circle and everything is the same as before. Even though Brett has new awareness, her life is still the same—she is going back to Mike. Robert will also go back to Frances and his old life with even less self-esteem.

Jake, though, has changed. Regardless of how she leads him on, by the end he realizes being with her is an inaccessible dream. When she says they would have been good together, he replies that is "pretty to think so." He realizes this is a delusion. Jake's conversion is complete.

Study Questions

1. Where do the three men decide to travel together?
2. Who avoids Jake when he is checking out?
3. Why can't Mike pay for drinks?
4. Why doesn't Jake want to go to Paris with Bill?
5. Where does Jake go in Spain?
6. What kind of race is going on in San Sebastian?
7. Where does Brett ask Jake to come?
8. Why is Brett upset?
9. Besides Brett, how many women has Romero been with?
10. Where are Brett and Jake at the end of the story?

Answers

1. Bill, Jake, and Mike travel together as far as Bayonne.
2. When Jake is checking out, Montoya avoids him because of his role in Romero and Brett's affair.
3. Mike cannot pay for the drinks because he is out of money.
4. Jake does not want to go to Paris because he does not want to party anymore.
5. In Spain, Jake goes to San Sebastian.
6. The Tour du Pays Basque bicycle race is being run in San Sebastian.
7. Brett contacts Jake to meet her in Madrid.
8. When Jake arrives, Brett is upset because Romero has left her.
9. Besides Brett, Romero has only been with two women.
10. At the end of the story, Brett and Jake are in a taxi in Madrid.

Suggested Essay Topics

1. Compare the bullfighters and bike racers. What is meant by, "They did not take the race seriously except among themselves." How does his relate to the "lost generation"?

2. Give reasons for Brett and Romero's breakup. How does this show growth for Brett? What does the quote, "It's sort of what we have instead of God," mean?

3. Explain Jake's comment, "Send a girl off with one man. Introduce her to another to go off with him. Now go and bring her back. And sign the wire with love. That was it all right." How does this relate to the final quote: "Isn't it pretty to think so." Does this show growth for Jake? What does it mean?

Sample Analytical Paper Topics

Topic #1

Show how Hemingway uses setting to demonstrate his characters' moral and ethical standards.

Outline

I. Thesis Statement: *Hemingway uses a variety of settings to demonstrate various characters' attitudes about life.*

II. Paris

    A. Excessive drinking

    B. No religion

    C. Idle rich

    D. Abnormal sexual practices

III. Pamplona

    A. Bullfighting

    B. Cathedrals along countryside

    C. *Aficiónados*

IV. Burguete

    A. Fishing

    B. Communing with nature

    C.   Harris

V.   San Sebastian

    A.   Relaxation

    B.   Swimming

    C.   Bicycle race

VI.   Madrid

    A.   All roads lead there

    B.   Comes to terms with Brett

    C.   Goes to Brett's rescue

Topic #2

Show how Stein's "lost generation" is represented in the novel. How does Hemingway feel about them?

Outline

I.   Thesis Statement: *By focusing on various characters' injuries, Hemingway shows the lack of productivity and morals of the "lost generation."*

II.   Jake

    A.   War injury

    B.   Impotent

    C.   Unable to satisfy his true love

III.   Brett

    A.   Lost love

    B.   Alcoholic

    C.   Cannot find/keep true love

    D.   In abusive relationships

IV.   Count Mippopolous

    A.   War injury

    B.   Self-satisfying

    C.   Shallow

V. Michael

    A. War injury

    B. Alcoholic

    C. Financially bankrupt

    D. Morally bankrupt

    E. Mean to Robert

Topic #3

Show how Hemingway uses religion to demonstrate Jake's code and his violation of it.

Outline

I. Thesis Statement: *Hemingway uses a religious framework to develop Jake's code and his violation of it.*

II. Fishing in Burguete

    A. Communion-like scene

    B. Appreciation of nature

    C. Simplicity of desires

III. Catholicism

    A. On train to Burguete

    B. Jake's praying

    C. Various cathedrals

    D. Jake's religion of record

IV. Pedro

    A. Priest figure

    B. Leader of three matadors

    C. *Aficiónado*

    D. Monastic room

V. Brett

    A. Mary Magdalene figure

    B.   Sees she deserves Mike, not Romero

    C.   Tries to pray for Romero

    D.   Unable to make inner conversion

VI. Montoya

    A.   Laying on of hands

    B.   Secret with Jake

    C.   *Aficiónado*

    D.   Disapproves of Jake's sin

VII. Bullfighting

    A.   Ritualistic

    B.   Spiritually awakening

    C.   Accompanied by extreme emotion

SECTION SIX

Bibliography

Quotations for *The Sun Also Rises* are taken from the following edition:

Hemingway, Ernest. *The Sun Also Rises.* New York: Scribner's Paperback Fiction, 1954.

Other Sources:

Lynn, David H. *The Hero's Tale.* "*The Sun Also Rises: Heroism of Innocence, Heroism of a Fallen World*" New York: St. Martin's Press, 1989, pp. 92–117.

Mizener, Arthur. *The Sense of Life in the Modern Novel.* Boston: Houghton Mifflin, 1964.

Reynolds, Michael S. *The Sun Also Rises (A Novel of the Twenties).* Boston: Twayne Publishers, 1988. pp. ix–4.

WEBSTER'S Ninth New Collegiate Dictionary. Merriam-Webster Inc. Springfield, Massachusetts. 1983 ed.

THE BEST TEST PREPARATION FOR THE

AP
ADVANCED
PLACEMENT
EXAMINATION

ENGLISH
Literature & Composition

by Pauline Beard, Ph.D. • Robert Liftig, Ed.D. • James Malek, Ph.D. •
James Maloney, M.A. • Joanne Miller, M.A. • Peter Trenouth, M.A. • Mattie Williams, M.A.

6 Full-Length Exams

➤ Every question based on the current exams
➤ The ONLY test preparation book with detailed explanations to every question
➤ Far more comprehensive than any other test preparation book

Includes a COMPREHENSIVE AP COURSE REVIEW,
emphasizing all areas of literature & composition found on the exam

REA *Research & Education Association*

Available at your local bookstore or order directly from us by sending in coupon below.

REA's **Test Preps**
e **Best in Test Preparation**

A "Test Preps" are far **more** comprehensive than any other test preparation series
:h book contains up to **eight** full-length practice exams based on the most recent exams
:ry type of question likely to be given on the exams is included
swers are accompanied by **full** and **detailed** explanations

REA has published over 60 Test Preparation volumes in several series. They include:

:ed Placement Exams (APs)

s AB & Calculus BC
try
:er Science
 Language & Composition
 Literature & Composition
an History
ment & Politics
s
logy
 Language
States History

e Level Examination gram (CLEP)
an History I
s & Interpretation of
ature
 Algebra
an College Composition
 Examinations
 Growth and Development
:tory Sociology
es of Marketing

Subject Tests
an History

try

.
re

SAT II: Subject Tests (continued)
Mathematics Level IC, IIC
Physics
Spanish
Writing

Graduate Record Exams (GREs)
Biology
Chemistry
Computer Science
Economics
Engineering
General
History
Literature in English
Mathematics
Physics
Political Science
Psychology
Sociology

ACT - American College Testing Assessment

ASVAB - Armed Service Vocational Aptitude Battery

CBEST - California Basic Educational Skills Test

CDL - Commercial Driver's License Exam

CLAST - College Level Academic Skills Test

ELM - Entry Level Mathematics

ExCET - Exam for Certification of Educators in Texas

FE (EIT) - Fundamentals of Engineering Exam

FE Review - Fundamentals of Engineering Review

GED - High School Equivalency Diploma Exam (US & Canadian editions)

GMAT - Graduate Management Admission Test

LSAT - Law School Admission Test

MAT - Miller Analogies Test

MCAT - Medical College Admission Test

MSAT - Multiple Subjects Assessment for Teachers

NTE - National Teachers Exam

PPST - Pre-Professional Skills Tests

PSAT - Preliminary Scholastic Assessment Test

SAT I - Reasoning Test

SAT I - Quick Study & Review

TASP - Texas Academic Skills Program

TOEFL - Test of English as a Foreign Language

:ESEARCH & EDUCATION ASSOCIATION
 Ethel Road W. • Piscataway, New Jersey 08854
none: (908) 819-8880

Please send me more information about your Test Prep Books

ame _____

ddress _____

ity _____ State _____ Zip _____